DIPLOMACY FAR REMOVED

A REINTERPRETATION OF THE U.S. DECISION TO OPEN

DIPLOMATIC RELATIONS WITH JAPAN

By

Bruce Makoto Arnold

A Senior Thesis Submitted to

the Department of East Asian Studies

In Partial Fulfillment of the

Bachelor of Arts degree

THE UNIVERSITY OF ARIZONA

MAY 2005

ABSTRACT

Arnold, Bruce Makoto, <u>Diplomacy Far Removed: A Reinterpretation of the U.S. Decision to Open Diplomatic Relations with Japan</u>. Bachelor of Arts (East Asian Studies), May 2005, University of Arizona, Tucson, Arizona.

On the morning of April 28, 1849, the USS *Preble*, a sloop of war commanded by James Glynn, weighed anchor and sailed away from Nagasaki harbor. On board were fourteen men from the whaler *Lagoda* who had been held for over a year by Japanese authorities. Upon interrogation, the men stated that they were physically mistreated by the Japanese. Two years earlier, sailors from the whaler *Lawrence,* who were also forced onto Japanese shores and held captive, reported similar mistreatment. The story of these events comprised over fifty pages of the original Senate report used to persuade the United States Congress to approve a naval expedition to Japan.

This study seeks to clarify the impact of the stories of the *Lawrence* and *Lagoda* on the decision to send the U.S. mission to Japan. After examining the actual narratives of the sailors and comparing them with Japanese reports in order to ascertain a factual baseline, the study examines the reaction to the *Lawrence* and *Lagoda* by prominent businessmen, naval officers, and politicians. Then, the reaction to the *Lawrence* and *Lagoda* is placed in the contextual framework of prevailing mid-nineteenth century American social, cultural, and legal attitudes in order to show that humanitarian concerns were, indeed, a prime consideration for sending the Perry mission to Japan.

TABLE OF CONTENTS

INTRODUCTION

It is impossible to study modern Japanese history without examining the Unite States' momentous mission to Japan in 1853.[1] The consequences of Commodore Matthew C. Perry's bold entrance into Edo Bay and his audacious diplomacy forced Japan to acknowledge that it was a reluctant member of a world that was expanding without regard to its objections. What followed—upheaval, unrest, and civil war—left Japan struggling to define its place in the world vis-à-vis mercantile powers that were all too willing to take advantage of its worldly inexperience.

Although I had always assumed that the insatiable American appetite for maritime expansion was sufficient explanation for the 1853 mission, a Japanese history class lecture gave me reason to reconsider. The lecture had referred to the New Bedford whalers *Lawrence* and *Lagoda*, whose crews, for differing reasons, found themselves on the shores of Japan in the late 1840s. Incarcerated for an extended period of time, they reported that they were treated inhumanely. Claims of mistreatment included excessive exposure to the elements, confinement in cages too small to allow the men to stand, forced sacrilegious acts against Christian religious icons, and severe beatings. These stories were widely disseminated in the print media and were eventually placed in Congressional documents that were used to justify the naval expedition to Japan.

⋆ This study was made possible, in part, by a generous University of Arizona Honors Research Grant awarded in 2002 and by a travel stipend provided by Peter and Elaine Given of Hamilton, New Zealand.

After Perry's return in 1854, controversy arose over the real purpose of the mission. Whigs, the party of then-President Millard P. Fillmore and the party to which the majority of the New England seafaring community belonged, defended the mission's goal, which was, they argued, to help bring Japan into compliance with "Natural Law," which strictly prohibited the type of treatment the whalers received. Fillmore's letter to the Emperor of Japan specifically mentioned the plights of the whalers of the *Lawrence* and *Lagoda*, as well as the inhospitable reception received by the private American merchant ship *Morrison* in 1837. Democrats, on the other hand, criticized the use of the sailors' plights as a simple political ruse, and argued that commerce alone should dictate the necessity of such missions.[2] This question was allowed to go unresolved and did not receive considerable attention from historians until the 1930s. These historians, most of whom were influenced by the Progressive movement, tended to favor a "commerce first" explanation that reflected their general disdain for profit-based political motivations. As a result, they published detailed studies and analyses of the underlying commercial motivation for the mission and its outcome.[3]

Progressive historians' interpretations were based on the observation that nearly all of the businessmen, naval officers, and government officials who proposed missions to Japan had at least some commercial sympathies, which was a natural consequence of America's expanding interests in oceanic trade and its reliance on the whale for products such as oil to heat lamps and light streets, and bones, used for furniture and ornamentation. However, since the establishment of the "commerce first" explanation and its subsequent acceptance, historians have continued to study American ethics, culture, and society as it related to mid-nineteenth century political and commercial discourse. If applied to the Perry mission, these recent studies are helpful in deepening our understanding of this momentous event.

This study however, seeks, through the study of primary source material and recent scholarship, to re-evaluate the Perry mission in the context of the socio-political and socio-religious values which also drove U.S. foreign policy during the mid-nineteenth century. It concedes that commercial concerns were a prime motivating force behind the Perry mission, but argues, on the other hand, that one cannot ignore the context of nineteenth-century ethics or socio-political and socio-religious mores, because to do so denies that the expedition was governed by the overall ethical and moral constructs of that age. Most scholarship surrounding the Perry mission centers on the view that commercial and humanitarian concerns are mutually exclusive ideals; in contrast, I argue here that such an either/or position neglects the larger context in which the mission was carried out. Recent historical studies of mid-nineteenth century ethics and mores suggest that commerce, religion, and notions of international law were more inclusive than had been previously thought. This recent scholarship suggests that the Perry mission was not simply an exercise in commercialism or a merely a demonstration of national self-aggrandizement on the part of the United States, but that Western politicians' and merchants' worldview assumed the existence of laws of nature that governed men and governments. This mindset linked commercial and humanitarian concerns, justifying, in their minds, the goal of opening Japan, even forcibly, if necessary, to commercial and diplomatic relations with the Western world.

CHAPTER I

RECONSIDERING "COMMERCE FIRST"

For any historian who examines the relationship between the Pacific Ocean and the United States since the end of the Revolutionary War, the strategic position of Japan to America's commercial interests becomes immediately clear. As early as the first two decades of the nineteenth century, New England whaling vessels hunted in the South Pacific and steadily tracked their prey northward until they plied their trade directly off the frigid waters of Hokkaido. Later, as trade with China also steadily increased, businessmen, and even Perry himself, envisioned using one of Japan's islands as a stop along the Great Circle Route to provide fuel for coal-hungry steamships on route to trading ports in East Asia. As America's presence in the Pacific Ocean expanded, naval officers, charged to ensure the safety of American merchant marines, whale ships, and cargo, had proposed missions to Japan, in an effort to facilitate trade and to protect and the growing lifeblood of American Pacific commerce. These proposals, all of which naturally related to private maritime economic considerations, led many historians to view America's continual encroachment on the Japanese as primarily motivated by an insatiable need to expand and influence overseas trade.

Perhaps it is no surprise that the commercial considerations for the mission received the greatest attention from historians since interest in Japan was relatively sparse until it began to assert itself on the world stage after its participation in the First World War and its subsequent invitation to the Paris Peace Conference and its inclusion into the League of Nations. As early as 1907, a lecture given by F. H. Hamlin to the Canandaigua (New York)

Scientific Association aimed to "rescue temporarily from the fast advancing waves of oblivion…one most delicate mission" (in reference to commander James Glynn's mission to Japan to free the men of the whale ship *Lagoda*).[4] Hamlin drew his facts, in part, from "the dusty archives of the Navy Department," which housed "many forgotten records of notable events."[5]

Subsequent investigations into the opening of Japan coincided with what historian William Adam Borst, in 1972, described as the "devil theory" of history, which was written by "Progressive historians and their intellectual heirs during the Great Depression" and "treated the merchant and his industrial descendents with disdain, if not blatant contempt."[6] Borst found that these historians "greatly distorted the historical balance" and "have too often prescribed a condemnation of the merchant legacy as a panacea to explain away all social and economic ills."[7] Borst argued that the Progressive legacy "dealt irreparable harm" to the study of the "natural economic impulse to advance one's financial situation through commercial activity."[8] Merchants such as Aaron H. Palmer and Charles King who, Borst noted, "provided the energy and the visions" that led America's Japan policy, were driven by the "dynamic environment of expansion in America that had permeated all phases of American life."[9] The "dynamic expansion," Borst identifies does not mean commercial aspirations alone, it also refers to the American cultural and religious identity that grew out of internal movements such as the Second Great Awakening and the emergence of eighteenth century humanism and interpretations of imported Victorian ideals. Borst alludes to motivations larger than the individual as responsible for an expressed "moral imperative" and "religious imagination."[10]

Borst suggests that further reinterpretation of the motivations behind the Perry mission must reach beyond the boundaries of mercantilism and imperialism to include the non-commercial justifications cited by those who proposed, planned, and implemented Perry's mission to Japan. One such justification cited in Fillmore's letter to the Japanese emperor, delivered to Japanese officials in 1853, was an American desire "to live in peace and friendship" with Japan, but it was feared that a friendship could not exist, unless Japan ceased "to act towards Americans as if they were her enemies."[11] The events referred to were the mistreatment of crewmembers of two whaling vessels—the *Lawrence* and the *Lagoda* and constitute one such non-commercial justification for the mission.

Historian Helen Humeston's 1981 study of the origins of U.S. official policy toward Japan also challenged the assumption that only economic considerations—mostly private—drove the mission to Japan. She questioned the consensus among scholars that a select group of intrepid people acted ahead of American foreign policy, while politicians often merely served to validate the successes of an "ad-hoc and incremental" Japan policy, rather than to form it.[12] In place of this common explanation that she found centered on a "wholly…American economic set of causes…in isolation from contemporaneous trends in foreign policy," she suggested that "the reopening of Japan [was] a diplomatic maneuver designed to achieve concrete purposes in the United States' global strategy."[13] Humeston proposed a new approach to the study of the Perry mission, one that "[placed] the issue in a broader perspective and [re-evaluated] it in the light of recent interpretations of United States diplomatic policy."[14] She argued that the U.S. policy toward Japan reflected Americans' perceptions of their own "self-identity, self-interest, and world view."[15]

How exactly did reports of sailors' and whalers' mistreatment connect with Americans' "world view," "self-interest," and "sense of self," and evolve into a need to protect the well-being of those who plied their oceanic trade ever closer and closer to Japan? How, too, can notions such as "self-interest" reflect humanitarian concerns? Answering these questions helps place the Perry mission in a larger context that includes cultural and socio-religious factors in nineteenth-century American commercial expansion. In addition, this answer would be a timely addition to recent scholarship that attempts to bridge the gap between nineteenth-century economics and American social and cultural norms and to shed light on the prevailing attitudes of the time.

One area that has been the subject of contemporary scholarly revision is that of the Christian evangelical sentiment that swept through the nation during the Second Great Awakening. In the mid-nineteenth century, the influence of both revivalist-born Christian optimism and Victorian propriety greatly affected Americans. People who identified with Christian values and ethics perceived their fates as tied together with the same Providence that had carried their young nation to the edge of world preeminence. Furthermore, many believed that it was America's destiny to share its providential gifts with the rest of the world. If viewed within this larger context, the mission to Japan may be seen as an outgrowth of this widespread social movement.

Historian Mark Noll argues that Christian attitudes greatly influenced nineteenth-century commerce and that we have only recently begun to identify the many ways this influence was applied to commercial ethics and mores.[16] His study of Americans' attitudes during the mid-nineteenth century found that religion greatly influenced secular perceptions of public and private morality. The excitement arising from U.S. territorial and oceanic expansion gave rise to an American view of commerce that was directly linked to Divine Providence. The Perry mission, a product of both commercial, and the less-studied socio-religious and socio-political concerns, serves to illustrate the prevailing belief that there was a profound connection between Christian values and monetary gains that would arise from the proper and heartfelt application of those values. These Christian-inspired values, tied directly to the Victorian concept of the interaction between God and nature, evolved from early attempts to define laws that integrated Greek philosophical thought on the divine, nature, and man's ability to develop and evolve. Known as Natural Law, these tenets were absorbed into Christian thought through the Roman adoption of Greek legal philosophies.

Linked strongly to Christian thought, the ideals defined by the concept of Natural Law (also known as the Law of Nations or International Law) were not only a driving force behind mid-nineteenth century Christian revivalism, but were the foundation of U.S. political and commercial constructs and formed the backbone of American and European international diplomatic policy. For a large majority of the nineteenth-century policymakers, Natural Law, combined with prevalent Christian ideals, formed a wholly justifiable moral and ethical base from which to launch the mission to Japan. Policymakers believed that the Natural Law was an inductive and fundamental set of moral and ethical standards. If an individual or nation adhered to these standards, positive outcomes, such as commercial success, were its natural results. By ignoring the impact of Natural Law, historians have failed to acknowledge individual proponents of the mission whose interests in the mission were exemplary for their day. Men such as President Millard P. Fillmore have often been overlooked in favor of those individuals who appear to justify the "commerce first" explanation. In order to understand how the humanitarian aspects of Natural Law affected the Perry mission directly, it is important to fully understand how the mistreatment of the crews of the *Lawrence* and *Lagoda* was represented to the American people.

NOTES FOR CHAPTER I

1. This study is aware that the mission's first commander was John H. Aulick, however, for the sake of brevity, the mission will be credited, if, in rhetoric only, to Matthew C. Perry.

2. "The Japan Expedition and its Results," *The United States Democratic Review* 32, no 1 (1853): 66-7 and "Japan—the Expedition," *The American Whig Review* 15, no. 90 (1852): 508.

3. Helen Humeston, "Origins of America's Japan Policy, 1790-1854" (Ph.D. diss., University of Minnesota, 1981), 2 and passim.

4. F.H. Hamlin, "A forgotten naval expedition and something of its commander, James Glynn" (Paper read before the Canandaigua Scientific Association, Canandaigua, New York, October 1907), 1. This document, discovered at the Naval Historical Center in Washington, D.C., as far as the author can determine, has never been referenced in any historical work. The document, crumbling and in need of repair, is invaluable, because Hamlin claims to have spoken to men who served with Glynn and under Glynn's command. If true, this document contains the only first-hand accounts of the officer outside of the reports he wrote to his post commander David Geisinger after his visit to Nagasaki in 1849.

5. Ibid, 2.

6. William Allan Borst, "The American Merchant and the Genesis of Japanese-American Commercial Relations, 1790-1858" (Ph.D. diss., Saint Louis University, 1972), 1-2. In his 1972 dissertation at the Saint Louis University, Borst wrote about American merchants' influence on American Japan policy from 1790 to 1858. It represents, in my estimation, an initial attempt of a historian to replace "blame" with understanding as it relates to the Perry mission. However, Borst continues to approach America's Japan policy from the point of view that commercial considerations and contemporary humanitarian values were largely separate concerns, which hinders his final outcome.

7. Ibid, 2.

8. Ibid.

9. Ibid, 230.

10. Ibid, 17, 64. Borst intensely studies Palmer, King, and Townsend Harris in his study.

11. Letter drafted by Edward Everett in the name of Millard Fillmore, to be delivered to the Emperor of Japan through the commander of the mission, Commodore Matthew C. Perry. A copy can be found in *Correspondence Relative to the Naval Expedition to Japan,* United State Senate, 33rd Congress, 2nd Session, Senate Executive Document 34, 9-11.

12. Humeston, 2.

13. Ibid, 3.

14. Ibid, 2.

15. Ibid, 3.

16. Mark A. Noll, "Introduction," in *God and Mammon: Protestants, Money, and the Market, 1790-1860* ed. Mark A. Noll (New York: Oxford University Press, 2002), 7.

CHAPTER II

THE ORDEALS OF THE CREWS OF THE *LAWRENCE* AND *LAGODA*

The anchors of the *Equator* and *Balaena* plunged into the waters off Honolulu in 1819, signaling the beginning of the American whaling fleet's advance toward Japan.[1] Although merchant ships had used Hawaii as a stopover on their way from North America to Canton for many years, whalers were the first to utilize it as a permanent supply depot. By 1823, sixty ships had called on the islands' ports, and by 1844, over four hundred ships were anchoring there annually. New England's cultural influence quickly spread throughout the islands, turning many ports into a near mirror-image of a typical East Coast whaling village.[2]

As the more popular southern whaling areas became depleted in the 1830s, the bulk of the American fleet concentrated on the more inhospitable waters surrounding Japan. Sperm whales off the waters of Japan attracted the attention of the *Maro* in 1821, and soon thereafter, thirty more ships followed. By 1847, 177 American whalers frequented the North Pacific. The *Seaman's Friend of Honolulu* noted the proximity of the fleet to Japan when it reported that "not scores, but hundreds of vessels spread their canvas within full view of the coast."[3] Given their proximity to the islands, meetings between the whalers and the Japanese were inevitable. When the two came into contact, the results were often less than amicable.

Western vessels that approached Japan in the nineteenth century did so without the blessings of Japan's ruling class. Since the mid-seventeenth century, the Japanese viewed contact with Westerners as a potentially dangerous act. Although powerful Japanese lords had attempted to attract Western trade for much of the sixteenth century, the powerful Tokugawa clan that had unified the country sought to limit the war making capabilities of rival warlords who could use firearms to gain a military advantage. After peasants, who claimed to be Christian converts, revolted in Kyushu in 1637, the Tokugawa leaders adopted a policy of near-seclusion. After this, trade only existed with the Koreans, who were limited to trading with the Japanese on Tsushima Island, the Chinese, who were limited to trade in Nagasaki and the Ryukyus, and the Dutch, who were restricted to a small manmade island in Nagasaki harbor.

Early American Encounters with Japan—the Eclipse and Manhattan

Although American merchant ships had been in constant contact with Japan since the United States was founded, these were almost always ships that were re-flagged and carried cargo for the Dutch during times of European conflict. Ships such as the *Margaret* (1801), *Samuel Smith* (1802), *Rebecca* (1803), *America* (1806), and *Mount Vernon* (1807) stood in place of besieged Dutch vessels and put in at Nagasaki.[4] These ships encountered no problems with Japanese officials since their true nationality was not known.

The *Eclipse* (1807) was the first U.S. vessel to run afoul of Japanese officials. The ship, "chartered at Canton by the Russian American company for a voyage to Kamchatka and the Northwest Coast," was flying Russian colors as it entered port.[5] It had encountered a storm that damaged its fresh water barrels, necessitating the need to stand in at Nagasaki for repairs. The Dutch superintendent informed the ship's captain that he should lower the flag and not to reveal his Russian supercargo.

The Japanese had, in fact, turned away several Russian ships that had come to Japan seeking trade beginning in 1792.[6] Japan feared that Russia would use Christian teachings to subvert the peasantry and create unrest, leading to an outright revolt.[7] Subsequent Russian ships that came to Japan, regardless of the pretext, were sent away and warned not to return. In one instance, informing the Russians that they were not to approach Japanese waters, because Japanese law stipulated that they would "destroy any ship from a country not maintaining diplomatic ties that is cast upon our shores, and we must permanently incarcerate its crew."[8]

Although the *Eclipse* was surrounded by guard boats in Nagasaki harbor and told to leave, it suffered no harm, and was repaired and re-supplied before being towed out to sea and sent on its way. The next two ships to visit Japan did not fare as well. The reports from those ships' crews were printed in the media and began to open the eyes of Americans to Japan.

According to a new edict drafted in 1825, all foreign ships approaching the coastline should be driven off with gunfire, and if "circumstances dictate," the vessel was to be destroyed.[9] The first American vessel to test the edict was the *Morrison*, which was owned by the American firm Olyphant and Company. On July 30, 1837, it arrived off Uraga Bay, carrying seven Japanese castaways.[10] As the ship approached shore, the local magistrate ordered shore batteries to open fire, causing the *Morrison* to withdraw. Japanese cannons were moved up shore where they began to fire on the vessel again the following morning. When ball struck the ship, she pulled out of range. Upon reaching Kagoshima, the crew attempted to repatriate the castaways, but they were fired upon once again. The *Morrison* eventually returned to Macao, and the castaways never returned home.

Official Japanese policy changes in 1842 somewhat lessened the harsh policy set forth in 1825.[11] Consequentially, the U.S. ship *Manhattan*, which had picked up twenty-one Japanese castaways in 1845, was welcomed somewhat differently. The captain of the *Manhattan* decided to repatriate the castaways near Edo, but the latter were fearful that they would be shelled when they approached the shore. They persuaded the captain to land two pairs of them in two remote locations, from where they would explain their plight to officials. Eventually, the *Manhattan* was allowed to land near Uraga to repatriate the remaining castaways. Although the ship was not shelled, it was surrounded by a thousand boats carrying armed men, and, upon its departure, was instructed to warn other vessels that if any further like attempts were made to repatriate castaways, the ships would be "treated rigorously."[12]

These types of stories affected large segments of the American population that relied on the ocean for their livelihood or sustenance. In his study of the American whaling industry, Walter S. Tower estimated that between the years 1835 and 1855, whaling directly provided for the livelihoods of seventy thousand Americans.[13] During that period, over 600 American ships sailed the world's oceans in search of the whales that accounted for products valued at over $8,000,000 annually.[14] Local newspapers kept whaling communities involved in the lives of their denizens at sea, while national publications such as *Littell's Living Age* and *Niles National Register*, along with religiously-oriented periodicals such as the *Sailors' Magazine and Naval Journal*, reached a wider American audience.

The earlier encounters with Japan had been enough to inform the seafaring community of the possible consequences if their ships came into contact with Japan. Up to that point, however, the stories surrounding Japan lacked a personal perspective. The stories from the crews of the next two ships to encounter Japan would give maritime communities a new perspective.

The Lawrence

The first incident involving the mistreatment of sailors involved a whaling ship named the *Lawrence*. There were two widely published accounts of the incident. The first, written by second mate George Howe, appeared in *Singapore Free Press* on January 6, 1848 and subsequently was reprinted in the *Straet's Times, Extra* on February 14. The article was further reprinted in Senate Documents of the Thirty-Second Congress, the document used to argue the need for a mission to Japan. The second account, which appeared after the decision to send a mission to Japan had already been made, was the result of an interview with ship's carpenter Murphy Wells. It appeared in the *New York Times* on June 15, 1852.[15]

On May 27, 1846, the New York whaler *Lawrence* encountered a gale off the Kurile Islands. The ship, along with a whale tied to its side, drifted until evening when it struck rocks and broke apart. Although most, if not all of the crew, managed to escape the stricken vessel in three launches, only one was eventually left drifting in the north Pacific.[16] The surviving craft was manned by the *Lawrence's* second mate, George Howe, its carpenter, Murphy Wells, and six other crewmembers, one of whom died on the third day and was buried at sea.[17] On the third day of June, the crew spotted the island of Etorofu (now Iterup) and landed at a place called Toshimoi, where the men killed and ate a seal along with some grass that they found growing along the beach.[18] Afterwards, the men began to scout the area, leaving one man to guard the boat. Three miles inland, they discovered a bamboo cottage and immediately called out to attract the attention of any inhabitants. They waited for an hour, but encountered no one.

While the reconnoitering party was away, two Ainu happened upon the launch. After a brief attempt to communicate with its caretaker, they hurried to the nearby town of Rubetsu to inform the local authorities. The next morning the crew encountered the guards that had been dispatched to investigate. The guards rapidly approached them with swords and spears, and as they drew close the crew fell to its knees. Howe felt that he would have been struck down by a guard's sword if his hand had not been "held back by an old man who stood behind him."[19] Through gestures the crew was able to communicate that they were hungry, but could not convey either their nationality or that of their ship.[20] After providing the weakened men with rice and fish, the Japanese motioned to the crewmen that they were to leave. The launch was hardly an ocean-going vessel, and after Howe indicated this to the guards, they were taken to Rubetsu. Howe believed that if the crewmen had tried to escape en route, they would have been killed. It is at Rubetsu that the crew began a long period of confinement.

Murphy Wells testified that the sailors were "were thrust into a prison cage, made similar to those in which wild beasts are kept for exhibition." Howe concurred, reporting that they were placed in a "small cell" and kept under constant guard. The crew was questioned every day as to their nationality, religion, "and every other particular that could be thought of."[21] Once, the sailors were given sake before their interview, which Howe speculated was a ploy to make their tongues both wet and loose. About the same time, all of the men became sick; this, combined with the "miserable situation" they were in and the "bad treatment" and "frequent" beatings and insults they received from the guards made them give up hope of ever surviving their imprisonment.[22]

On May 31, 1847, the arrival of fair weather and a 700 *koku* vessel allowed for the removal of the crew to Nagasaki.[23] The Japanese entourage accompanying the sailors included fourteen solders, a physician, seven servants, and a censor.[24] Once they set sail, the castaways were not allowed to step foot on deck, "breathe fresh air or see the light" for a period of "four months."[25] The ship arrived off Nagasaki on August 19, where the men were given a preliminary examination aboard ship.

The next day, the men were taken to the local magistrate in "a box, the lid of which was fastened down upon us."[26] Japanese records of this first extensive interview, taken through Dutch interpreters, indicate that the crew was asked such questions as their names, ages, nationalities, and familial composition.[27] Howe believed that they were questioned primarily to determine if they were English, and believed if they would have admitted to being so, they "would have all been killed."[28] Wells' account builds on this, indicating that the Japanese, thinking the men were English, threatened to cut off their heads.[29] During the interview, the sailors were made to spit and trample upon "a cross bearing the image of [the] Saviour."[30] Officers' epaulettes, one set American, the other British, were presented to the men who were asked to indicate which was from their country.[31]

Another meeting was scheduled soon after and in attendance was the English-speaking Dutch *opperhoofd*(superintendent), Joseph Henrij Levyssohn, who reportedly said that "if there are any [English] among you, you had better not say any thing about it."[32] Continuing, he confirmed their identities and asked the castaways to recount their story of the shipwreck. Following this interview, the Japanese sent a detailed account of the queries to the *bakufu* and asked if the prisoners should be set free and if their possessions should be returned to them.[33]

While awaiting a reply, one of the sailors died. Howe claimed that the man tried to escape from prison saying that "he would rather die than suffer so much any longer," and was "inhumanely murdered by the Japanese" after he was caught."[34] Wells' story later corroborated this:

> one of our comrades...endeavored to make his escape, but was caught and taken back to prison in a dying state, owing to wounds inflected on him with some deadly weapon; there was a gash over his forehead which bled profusely. The poor fellow lived about six hours.[35]

In a message dated September 22, the *bakufu* replied to the local officials' queries that the whalers should be released to the Dutch when a ship was ready to depart.[36] After the men had spent seventeen months in captivity, they were finally delivered to Deshima, and sailed from Japan on October 27.

Appeals on the behalf of the sailors appeared almost immediately. Peter Parker, temporary charge at Canton, forwarded a copy of Howe's account to Secretary of State James Buchanan along with a plea asking that the President "at least secure from [the Japanese government] the exercise of hospitality and humane treatment to our unfortunate countrymen who may be wrecked upon that distant coast."[37] Parker further noted that during the time the *Lawrence* sailors were imprisoned, Commodore James Biddle was anchored near Edo to ascertain if Japanese ports would be opened to American trade. Murphy Wells, too, appealed to his readers, stating that "it is anxiously hoped the American Government will not suffer this treatment, but more particularly so sanguinary an act towards hapless shipwrecked American seamen to pass without ample retribution."

The Lagoda

The second widely reported incident began on June 5, 1848, when fifteen sailors of the whale ship *Lagoda* deserted near the island of Hokkaido, apparently to escape cruel treatment.[38]

Upon reaching the coast two days later, the men attempted to land, but were turned away by shore inhabitants. They made their way northward for three miles and encountered villagers who allowed them to land and provided them with food and water.[39] A local official allowed them to stay until the next advantageous wind arrived to take them away. The seamen were placed within a "screen fort," in order to prohibit their movement and limit their contact with the local inhabitants.[40] As an additional precaution, guards, who carried swords and matchlocks, were assigned to watch them.

Fair conditions prevailed on the following morning, and men were given rice and firewood and sent on their way. They proceeded southward and saw that the villagers along the shore were wary of their presence.[41] A few miles beyond where they first attempted to land, the men spotted a small boat and were invited to the village by a sailor.[42] There, they were placed in "three mat enclosures run up for their reception" and were told to wait there until the weather became fair.[43] The men decided to sail on the next morning, but were restrained by guards (who had first been dispatched from Mastumae) who explained to them that an officer wished to speak with them, and since their diminutive launch would not fair well out on the open sea a larger vessel would be dispatched in order to take them away from the island.[44] When the asked why they had come to Japan, the whalers lied and claimed that their ship had foundered, taking with it twenty of their crewmates. In preparation for their stay, the crew's luggage was carried on to shore, tagged, and placed into a village house. The men were kept under guard for five days, after which, surrounded by soldiers, they were escorted to a local prison.

Under constant guard, never being allowed to step foot outdoors, the men waited twenty days for the larger ship to arrive. They were finally informed that the vessel had not arrived and would be delayed another twenty days. But, again, after waiting, the men were then told that their release would not come until January. The men requested permission to leave in their own craft, but this was denied.

Having lost confidence in the Japanese, the men attempted two abortive escape attempts which exacerbated the tension between both the sailors and their captors. On the first attempt, Robert McCoy and John Bull broke through the roof of the toilet and escaped, but were captured when they stopped to request food in a nearby village. Upon their return to the prison, the group became rowdy, apparently spurred on by Bull, which prompted a guard to isolate him. Bull was then "nailed into a grated crib…too low for him to stand up… by himself, for ten days," which did little to encourage his silence.[45] When he disobeyed orders not to speak, "he was jammed at with a stick, to compel him to be quiet."[46] Days later McCoy and John Martin also forced their way through a roof, but were apprehended near the coast. Both of the men were placed in an isolated cage along with Bull (it is unclear whether this is the same cage or not).[47] There the three remained for twenty five days and were "fed though a hole just large enough to admit a cup."[48] Martin, unfazed by Bull's punishment, attempted to communicate with the others and was taken out and thrown to the ground where a guard then stood on him "bound his arms, and then raised him up and secured him to a post" and then beaten about the face and head with the "bight of a rope."[49]

Around the tenth of August, a larger vessel (a junk) came to take the men away, but much to their dismay, their confinement continued. The three escapees were placed below decks into separate cages that measured four by six feet, with a height of five feet. The other twelve men were placed in a second cage, twelve by ten feet and "high enough to stand up in."[50] Upon their arrival in Nagasaki on September 2nd, the sailors illogically tried to convince their captors to give them their old vessels so that they could try to sail for China.[51] They were told that they would be taken ashore, and form there, in six weeks they would be forwarded to Batavia (Jakarta) on a Dutch ship.[52]

The men were questioned on board the junk, and then taken to the "town-house of Nagasaki" in "cago or chairs."[53] Once there, the men were ordered to stomp on a crucifix. McCoy testified his belief that if he did not comply, he would be put "in an iron house, from which death would be his only exit."[54] It appears that this punishment may have been only imagined, because one of the sailors who refused to step on the artifact was pushed and pulled until he was "forcibly fixed by his guard upon it."[55] Once inside, the men were made to squat down on the mats before the *bugyo's* (magistrate) approach.

The *bugyo* began what would become a series of interrogations, confinements, and escape attempts that widened the gap of mistrust and misunderstanding between the men of the *Lagoda* and the Japanese. Because of the late hour, only the most cursory examination was held, during which the sailors continued claim that they were shipwreck survivors.[56] The men were sent to a local temple, which contained a room surrounded by a fence some thirty feet high, outside of which was another wall eight to ten feet high.[57] A guard was placed in the room, separated from the whalers by a grating. A day or two later, the men were taken back to the residence of the *bugyo* and questioned in greater detail.

By this time, McCoy and Boyd felt they had learned enough Japanese to suspect that the interpreter, Moriyama, was not translating their testimony properly.[58] After making this known, the interrogation was adjourned until the following day when questioning resumed with the Dutch *opperhoofd* (superintendent) Joseph Henrij Levyssohn acting as interpreter. The Japanese pressed the crew for answers as to why the *Lagoda* had been in Japanese waters. The crew maintained that the *Lagoda* had come for no other reason than to hunt whales, and that its catch was primarily used to make whale oil. They were asked if they had come to spy on Japan to which they again asserted that they had only come in search of whales. The next day, the sailors were again brought back for another round of questioning, which was finally concluded by Moriyama, who asserted that he believed that they were there as spies "and came for no other purpose than to examine the country."[59]

It appears that by this time, the men, weary of their captivity and in such close proximity to the freedom of the Dutch factory in Deshima, began a series of desperate, if not bizarre, series of attempted escapes. McCoy, demonstrating his interminable defiance, tore off one of the boards of the inner fence and scaled the outer wall to gain his freedom. He hoped to reach a Dutch ship anchored in the harbor. After traveling all night, McCoy hid in the hills until four o'clock the next afternoon, when he made a break for the shore under the cover of a passing rainstorm. His quest for freedom ended in failure when he was caught and taken back to the temple where he was interrogated. In particular, the Japanese questioned him about "his object in spying out the land."[60] In an effort to prevent any further escapes, the guards put him in stocks and tied him to the grating during the night. The next morning, he was taken to the governor's residence and was again questioned about being a spy. He explained that his purpose was not to spy, but only to escape captivity. After this, he was taken to a "common prison" in Nagasaki and kept apart from the others for three weeks.[61]

At the end of his term, the Dutch ship that symbolized freedom to McCoy set sail without him, leaving him so distraught that he refused to eat his rations. When the governor heard of this, he sent a representative to ascertain his disposition and then brought him to his residence. In the presence of Levyssohn and the other sailors, the governor reached a bargain with McCoy that if he would remain quiet, he would be returned to his shipmates, which he was four days later. During the meeting, Levyssohn assured the whalers that he had written the American counsel in Batavia. However, many of the men appeared unwilling to trust their freedom to anyone but themselves, and perpetrated another escape by burning a hole through the floor and then digging under the outer fence. Although the guards foiled the plan before everyone could get out, McCoy, Bull, and Boyd made for a thicket behind the temple and hid. Later, the men made their way to the sea, but were captured when they unwisely asked a peasant for some food. Although he acquiesced and welcomed them into his home, he ran to notify officials while they ate. The guards came quickly, shackled them, and took them back to the temple.[62] Not willing to risk another breakout, the guards tied the escapees' arms "up behind their backs so tight and high, that when the cords were removed, after four hours of suffering, the poor fellows could not let their hands down without assistance."[63] Afterwards, they were "fettered in large stocks, McCoy's being much the heaviest, (about 300 lbs.,) and laid in the outer yard during the night: in the morning, wet with dew and stiff from constraint, they and all their companions were carried to the town-house."[64]

During their journey, the whalers warned the Japanese guards that the U.S. would not stand for its subjects being treated as they had been. Japanese "tauntingly" replied with,

> If any officers from your country come here, we'll serve them as we did the American commodore last year, who was knocked down at Yedo by a soldier. If the Americans took no notice of that, why should they look after you, who are only poor sailors? You are here now and can't help yourselves. If their ships come here, our priests will blow them to pieces.[65]

The commodore they spoke of was James Biddle, who had anchored off Uraga Bay in July 1846 with two American men-of-war to determine if a commercial treaty could be negotiated with the Japanese.

After another examination, the governor stated that he was becoming thoroughly convinced that the men were spies, given their numerous attempts to flee their confines and roam the countryside. In order ease his worries that the prisoners would again escape and to "secure" the men "from injuring themselves," he sent the group to the common prison in Nagasaki where they were confined to two "small cages" that were surrounded by a larger one.[66] One of the cages, measuring eighteen feet by eight, housed McCoy, Boyd, and Martin, while the rest were kept in a cage eighteen by twelve feet square. Although the men had no serious complaints about their confines at the temple, they noted that their new accommodations were "offensive, full of vermin and open to the weather, and to be entered only by crawling in."[67] The only furniture that they were given were "lousy mats and a small wash-stand."[68]

The added pressure of their captivity as well as the elements of the oncoming winter began to take its toll on the men. On December 17th, Maury, one of the Hawaiians, hung himself "by design, and not from aberration of mind."[69] His body was placed in a coffin and was buried in the same graveyard where the Dutch buried their dead.[70] Illness and exposure claimed the life of Ezra Goldthwait around Christmas.[71] In addition to the cold, the men claimed that the cages were at least partially exposed to rain and snow, and, that "no bedding, not even their own clothes," were given to the men of the group.[72] Although Goldthwait initially appeared to only be slightly ill, three days later he began to display symptoms such as deliria, "swelled and cracked tongue, pain in the stomach and frothing at the mouth."[73] The rapid onset of his sickness led the others to believe that he had been poisoned, and that the physician attending to him only served to make him worse.[74] He requested that the Bible he had smuggled in be returned to his family in Salem, Mass. Goldthwait, wearing only a shirt and trousers, lay on a quilt in his cage and beseeched the guards for a blanket, which was finally provided to him three days before he perished. He died on the 24th of January and was buried the following day. His shipmates were ridiculed when they asked to attend his funeral.[75] Soon after, John Walters began to display like symptoms.[76] His recovery was credited to the other crewmen, who would not let the doctor approach him. The guards had told him that the grave had already been dug, and that "the day appointed when they were to bury him."[77] Toward the end of their captivity, a convict was decapitated not far from the captives. Afterwards, the guards intimated that that, too, might be their fate.[78]

On April seventeenth, the prisoners heard the guns of the *Preble* as it approached the port. The guards told them that they were just "scaling" the guns of the port, but McCoy, who had begun to understand the Japanese language fairly well, learned that a ship had come to take them back. He was told that the captain of the American ship would have to wait for forty to fifty days for an answer to come back from Yedo because the governor had no real power to release the men. However, the men of the *Lagoda* were finally released on April 26th, thanks, in large part, to the recalcitrant stance and bold posturing by the commanding officer of the *Preble*, Lt. James Glynn.[79]

The Lawrence and Lagoda Incidents in a Maritime Context

The plight of the castaways from the *Lawrence* and *Lagoda* was by no means unique. Before these incidents, sailors who found themselves the unfortunate victims of the sea's ravages time and again were mistreated at the hands of foreign governments or by members of primitive tribes, pirates, and miscellaneous ruffians. Protection of such seamen fell well within the U.S. navy's purview, under which they "combated pirates, policed smuggling [and] protected and defended American lives, property, and trade…"[80] The navy's ships-of-the-line's peacetime missions "insured that American merchant ships remained unmolested, that American residents were not harassed, and that shipwrecked American sailors received friendly treatment."[81] If called to duty, these warships could carry out "punitive actions against people who had attacked American citizens or their interests."[82] Naval historian Tyler Dennett noted in his 1922 study of early American contacts with East Asia that the "treatment of the *Lagoda* survivors would have afforded sufficient excuse" for the United States (or, indeed, Glynn himself) to pursue "reprisals or war."[83] In historian Milton Offutt's 1928 study entitled, *The Protection of Citizens Abroad by the Armed Forces of the United States*, the author found "an unexpectedly large number of cases" where American naval officers demonstrated or applied force to "the troops or citizens of another nation within the jurisdiction of the foreign state."[84] Offutt's study cited fifteen separate occasions before Perry's mission to Japan and nearly double that number afterwards.

By the beginning of the 1840s, U.S. maritime interests were at an all-time high, and the protection of whalers and ships' crews was afforded strong consideration. The U.S. Pacific whaling fleet had been of particular interest for the navy since the second decade of the nineteenth century; by the 1840s, whaling interests were valued in excess of $40 million and employed sizable crews to man upwards of four hundred vessels valued at over $17 million.[85] Because of the great vastness of the ocean, protection of the fleet and "diplomacy could not be conducted without a continuous naval presence and frequent intervention by naval officers."[86] In order to protect their interests, industry leaders continually "pressed for and received naval support for whaling ships…in fact, the standing orders of virtually every American Commodore dispatched to the Pacific…carried specific instructions to protect whaling interests there."[87] Men such as Secretary of State Abel P. Upshur (1841-43) reinforced these positions during the period when he emphasized that the navy's "peacetime role…was the active protection of American commerce and citizens abroad." and that it "should move decisively to protect lawful commerce, to redress individual wrongs, and to prevent future transgressions."[88]

U.S. naval officers, following maritime convention and directives to protect ships and their crews, launched numerous punitive attacks against various people in order to protect American lives overseas. Admittedly, the officers' final solutions met with varying degrees of acceptance with the U.S. government.[89] In 1839, for example, Commodore George C. Read responded to reports that the merchant ship *Eclipse* had been attacked off the coast of Sumatra, resulting in the killing or wounding of many crewmembers, and the theft of its cargo of Spanish dollars and opium. Landing at the village of Quallah Batoo, Read "contacted the local rajah who promised to produce the culprits."[90] After two days of waiting, Read ordered the shelling of the village in Christmas day for one hour; although the town surrendered, the culprits were not handed over. Advancing to Mukkee, the pirates were still not surrendered, which compelled Read to shell and subsequently set fire the town. Read continued on to several villages along the Sumatran coast and extracted promises from the local rajahs that no further incidents would occur.

Lieutenant Charles Wilkes, who commanded the United States Exploring Expedition (1838-42) in the Pacific Ocean, was particularly concerned with the protection of merchant ships in the region and "attempted to investigate and punish those responsible" for "infringements on American trade or attacks on American whalers or seamen."[91] In 1840, when natives of the Fiji Islands attacked and killed two of his crew, Wilkes burned two villages, killed dozens of natives, and "demanded complete surrender from the local authorities."[92]

In 1843, Commodore Matthew Calbraith Perry himself participated in a punitive action against the village of Little Berebee on the Ivory Coast. Secretary of State Upshur ordered Perry to obtain reparations for an incident in 1841 involving the U.S. schooner *Mary Carver*, which had been plundered and its valuable cargo taken. On December 13, Perry's squadron of four ships anchored off the town and landed two hundred men. After negotiations with the local king broke down, Perry's ordered the burning of the village; the king was killed in the ensuing melee. After this show of force, Perry was able to extract assurances of protection for American lives and commerce by other area kings, who did not want to incur such wrath.

Conclusion

A nation's merchant marine fleet was (and still is) directly connected to the peacetime militarized navy. The latter's purpose was to protect both lives and commerce and to act as the diplomatic arm of the government when fast, direct communication was impossible due to the vast distances of the sea. Tradition and diplomatic instructions demanded that naval officers punish those responsible for any mistreatment of crews or for any harm caused by belligerents. In relation to the United States, the expanding cargo and whaling fleets in the Pacific along with American westward expansion obliged the government to place greater emphasis on using the navy to protect its human and commercial interests in the region.

Although most of the men who plied their trade on the world's oceans, such as those of the *Lawrence* and *Lagoda*, were not respecters of civil decorum or manners, this was irrelevant to those responsible for their well-being. Ruffians they may have been, but sailors were an integral portion of a maritime nation that utilized the ocean not only for the shipment of goods and people, but for the products that could be harvested from it. The skills they developed on the ocean, while not applicable to high society, were invaluable to the men around them and the ship they served. Without those men, the vessel they sailed was in peril, and so too were the people who depended directly on them for their sustenance.

The treatment received by the crewmen of the *Lawrence* and the *Lagoda* at the hands of their Japanese captors, was, in many ways, similar to many previous occurrences on the high seas. Prior to these events, the United States had followed long-established maritime tradition and the rules governing maritime law to prosecute and punish belligerents. Although nations with formal treaties based on maritime convention would preferably seek diplomatic settlements for these incidents, countries such as Japan that were outside of the maritime legal structure often received swift and harsh punishments for their perceived transgressions. In many ways, the incidents of the *Lawrence* and *Lagoda* and the associated American reactions represent restraint on the part of the United States government and commanders such as Glynn, who avoided commonly accepted practices of naval reprisals.

NOTES FOR CHAPTER II

1. A useful discussion of U.S. Pacific whaling can be found in: Foster Rhea Dulles, *Lowered Boats: A Chronicle of American Whaling* (New York: Harcourt, Brace, and Co., 1933), 240-245.

2. Ibid., 242.

3. *Seaman's Friend of Honolulu,* 1 December 1848.

4. Shunzo Sakamaki, *Japan and the United States: A Study of Japanese Contacts with and Conceptions of the United States and Its People Prior to the American Expedition of 1853-4* (Tokyo: Asiatic Society of Japan) 1939, 7-8.

5. Ibid., 9.

6. See Bob Tadashi Wakabayashi, *Anti-foreignism and Western Learning in Early-modern Japan: The New Thesis of 1825* (Cambridge, Mass.: Council on East Asian Studies, Harvard University, 1986), 59, 66, and passim.

7. See Ibid., 69-72 and passim. Religion was a historically important issue to the Japanese. In the early seventeenth-century, the Tokugawa house had began to eliminate any rivals to their power. Roman Catholics, and the nations that followed that religion, were targeted because the Pope was considered a higher authority than any Japanese. These nations were eventually excluded from all relationships with Japan. No nation felt this exclusion policy more than Portugal, because it was Jesuits who comprised the bulk of the Roman Catholic missionaries in Japan. Eventually, only the Protestant (not "Christian") Dutch were allowed to stay and trade in Japan, restricted to a small man-made island of Deshima, located in Nagasaki harbor.

8. Ibid., 66.

9. Ibid., 60.

10. For background information on this mission, see Sakamaki, 12-19. According to the exclusion party, anyone who left Japan for non-official reasons could not return—this included castaways.

11. Sakamaki, 19.

12. Ibid., 27.

13. Walter Sheldon Tower, *A History of the American Whale Fishery* (Philadelphia: The University of Pennsylvania Press, 1907), 51. At this time, there were approximately 2.7 million residents of the New England states and 20 million free and slave population total.

14. Ibid., 51.

15. Murphy Well's account was reprinted in Peter Duus, *The Japanese Discovery of America: A Brief History with Documents* (Boston: Bedford Books, 1997), 72-3. Duus' introduction to the article incorrectly states that the sailors "were not the victims of nature but mutineers who had sought refuge on the Japanese coast," a reference to the *Lagoda* incident, not the *Lawrence*.

16. Wells claimed that the crew waited until daylight and then lowered boats; all three remaining together until the night, when they separated and the other two were never seen again. Howe, on the other hand, claims that one of the boats was rent to pieces almost immediately, while the other, containing the captain, sailed off on its own and was never seen again.

17. *Official Documents Relative to the Naval Expedition to Japan.* United States Senate, 32nd Congress, 1st Session, Executive Document 59, 71.

18. Sakamaki, 37.

19. *Official Documents Relative to the Naval Expedition to Japan*, 71.

20. Ibid. and Sakamaki, 38.

21. *Official Documents Relative to the Naval Expedition to Japan*, 72.

22. Ibid. and Sakamaki, 40. According to Sakamaki, there may be some corroborating evidence to support the illness.

23. A koku is the equivalent of 5.12 bushels.

24. Sakamaki, 40. Official instructions made it clear that since the religion of the foreigners was not known, they should be carefully guarded when the boat was anchored so that they could not come into contact with the general population.

25. *Official Documents Relative to the Naval Expedition to Japan*, 72.

26. Ibid., 72. Although some have speculated that these were palanquins, this may have not been the case.

27. Sakamaki, 40.

28. Ibid., 42 and *Official Documents Relative to the Naval Expedition to Japan*, 72. Japanese documents admit that two of the seamen were questioned at length about their religion because they had been born in Portugal, but both had moved to the United States when they were very young.

29. Japan were especially concerned about the English since their victory in the first Opium War in 1839-1842. Until then, Japanese strategists had always assumed that Western nations had not the strength to conquer both China in Japan. They theorized that Japan, the weaker of the two states, would be attacked before China. However, England's relatively quick victory in China changed this perception. See Bob Tadashi Wakabayashi, "Opium, Expulsion, Sovereignty, China's Lessons for Bakumatsu Japan," *Monumenta Nipponica* 47, no. 1 (1992), 1-25.

30. *Official Documents Relative to the Naval Expedition to Japan*, 72 and Sakamaki, 42. Howe said that they had to spit on it and Wells and Howe said that this was "a print of the crucifixion." The Japanese fear of Christianity was so great that those suspected adherence would be ordered to trample on a Christian religious icon, usually a metal plate, known as a *fumie*, on which was stamped an image of a Crucifix or Mary holding baby Jesus. Those who refused to trample were often subjected to torture or sentenced to death.

31. *Official Documents Relative to the Naval Expedition to Japan*, 72.

32. Quoted in Ibid., 73. Even before the Opium Wars, the English were looked upon with suspicion by the Japanese. First, the English sent the *Return* in 1763, asking to open trade with the Japanese. However, the Dutch, in an effort to keep their trade monopoly, told Japanese officials that the English and Portuguese aristocracies were related through marriage, thus making England Christian (Roman Catholic), as well. Later, the it was well known to the Japanese that the English were often at war with the Dutch, and felt that the English would send spies to Deshima in order to prepare for an invasion. See also Wakabayashi, 64, 92.

33. Sakamaki, 42.

34. *Official Documents Relative to the Naval Expedition to Japan*, 73.

35. Although Sakamaki, 42, indicated that the Japanese version was corroborated by the *opperhooft*, he failed to note the Wells version of the deposition, taken years later, accurately corroborated Howe's story. Japanese reports claimed that he had died of dysentery on September 6, which was corroborated by Levyssohn, who said that the man had suffered from an illness to which he later succumbed.

36. Sakamaki, 42.

37. *Official Documents Relative to the Naval Expedition to Japan,* 69-70.

38. A summary of this story is found in a section of *Official Documents Relative to the Naval Expedition to Japan, 50-57,* entitled "Cruise of the U.S. Sloop-of-war Preble, Commander James Glynn, To Napa and Nangasacki [sic.]." Individual testimonies can be found in *Imprisoned American Seamen,* United States House of Representatives, 31st Congress, 1st Session, Executive Document, 84, 8-28.

39. Sakamaki, 51: Koisago was the first village, and Ishizaki the second

40. *Official Documents Relative to the Naval Expedition to Japan, 50.*

41. Sakamaki, 51: guards from Matsumae were already tracking them

42. Ibid.: Eramachi was this place

43. *Official Documents Relative to the Naval Expedition to Japan,* 51.

44. Sakamaki, 51: Indicates that the *Lagoda* men said that their boats were to small, but the *Lagoda* sailors' testimony indicates that the Japanese said they were too small.

45. *Official Documents Relative to the Naval Expedition to* Japan, 51.

46. Ibid.

47. *Imprisoned American Seamen,* 21: John Martin testified that a guard told them they would be set free in fifteen days.

48. *Official Documents Relative to the Naval Expedition to* Japan, 51.

49. Ibid: Both John Bull (18) and Martin (21) testified to this.

50. Ibid.

51. *Imprisoned American Seamen,* 20: Jacob Boyd testified that Moreyama told the sailors that the would be allowed to have their own boats in three days.

52. *Official Documents Relative to the Naval Expedition to Japan,* 52. The text adds "among other falsehoods."

53. Ibid. Also see Sakamaki, 52.

54. *Official Documents Relative to the Naval Expedition to Japan,* 52.

55. Ibid. and *Imprisoned American Seamen,* 20: Jacob Boyd testified that he was not willing to trample on it, but was forced to. First, he stepped on one edge, but was forced to go back and step on it with both feet. P. 21, James Martin testified that the same treatment was afforded to John Bull when he tried to bypass the crucifix. *Imprisoned American Seamen,* 24: Melcher Biffar testified that if he did not trample, the guards would assume that he was a Portuguese, which would be told to the governor.

56. Sakamaki, 52.

57. Ibid: Kofukuji temple

58. *Official Documents Relative to the Naval Expedition to Japan,* 52.

59. Ibid.

60. Ibid., 53.

61. Ibid.

62. *Imprisoned American Seamen,* 18: John Bull testified that they were first taken to "a sort of justice's office" where they were examined before being returned to the temple.

63. *Official Documents Relative to the Naval Expedition to Japan,* 53.

64. Ibid., 52. Melcher Biffar testified that the men wanted to "give them some covering," which was disallowed by the Japanese.

65. Ibid., 54 and *Imprisoned American Seamen,* 18, 20: John Bull testified that as the three escapees were taken out of their stocks, they told that Japanese guards that Americans would come to take vengeance on them for such cruelty. Both Boyd and Jabob Boyd testified that the city mentioned was "Yedo," which accurately reflects Biddle's location when he was shoved down by a Japanese guard.

66. *Official Documents Relative to the Naval Expedition to Japan,* 54.

67. Ibid., 54.

68. Ibid.

69. Ibid. Also listed as Maui, from Oahu, 25 in Sakamaki, 52.

70. *Imprisoned American Seamen,* 18: John Bull testified that when the sailors asked for permission to bury Mary, the Japanese "refused [them], laughing and scoffing at [their] request."

71. Sakamaki, 54. See also for a list of maladies the crew incurred.

72. *Imprisoned American Seamen,* 21: John Martin testified that they "made repeated applications for bedding and clothes, all which [the Japanese] refused."

73. *Official Documents Relative to the Naval Expedition to Japan,* 54.

74. Ibid. This is consistent with what the *Lawrence* sailors reported.

75. *Imprisoned American Seamen,* 18: John Bull claimed that Goldthwait, who had been in "perfect health, suddenly became sick, and entirely lost his appetite. He mouth became black, and throat and mouth very dry; he could not swallow, and had a singular wild appearance in the eyes....Immediately after his death, his body, about the pit of the stomach, became black and blue, probably within four hours afterwards." *Imprisoned American Seamen,* 21: John Martin concurred, adding that Goldthwait been "in great pain around the heart and stomach." *Imprisoned American Seamen,* 24: Biffar testified that as the Japanese took the box containing Goldthwait's body away, they were "making merry on the occasion."

76. Sakamaki, 52. Also known as Waters.

77. *Official Documents Relative to the Naval Expedition to Japan,* 54.

78. Ibid., 55.

79. Although there was probably little that could have been done to see the release of men of the *Lawrence* come sooner than a few months, several twists of fate conspired to ensure that they would spend the inordinate time of seventeen months in Japan. Most notable was the dangerous seas that had initially cast the men upon Japanese shores also prevented them from being transferred to more convenient facilities in a timely manner. The first report from the

district governor was sent to the *bakufu* concerning the sailors was dated on June 26, received no reply as to whether the sailors should be sent to Nagasaki. On September 3, a senior councilor to the shogun sent instructions that the men should be transported to Hokkaido in order to await passage to Nagasaki in the spring, but the message was sent too late, and never made it to Rebetsu. Although there is guarantee that the men would have reported better treatment if they were moved to Hokkaido, but the district governor was clearly concerned that he would not be able to properly care for the sailors. See Sakamaki, 39-40.

80. John H. Schroeder, *Shaping a Maritime Empire: The Commercial and Diplomatic Role of the American Navy, 1829-1861* (Westport, Conn.: Greenwood Press, 1985), 3.

81. Ibid., 6.

82. Ibid., 4.

83. Tyler Dennett, *Americans in East Asia: A Critical Study of the Policy of the United States with Reference to China, Japan, and Korea in the 19th Century* (New York: Macmillan Co., 1922), 251.

84. Milton Offutt, *The Protection of Citizens Abroad by the Armed Forces of the United States* (Baltimore: Johns Hopkins University Press, 1928), v.

85. Schroeder, *Shaping*, 62, 143.

86. Ibid., 9.

87. Ibid., 8.

88. Ibid., 70.

89. In November 1824, Commodore David Porter landed 200 men at the town of Fajardo, Puerto Rico to demand an apology from the mayor for imprisoning a naval officer. Porter was court-martialed for this act and subsequently resigned his commission to take up a similar post in the Mexican navy. See Schroeder, *Shaping*, 16.

90. See Schroeder, *Shaping*, 44-5.

91. Ibid., 68.

92. Ibid.

CHAPTER III

CHALLENGING HISTORICAL INTERPRETATIONS

With the Americans, as indeed with all Christian people, it is considered a sacred duty to receive with kindness, and to succor and protect all, of whatever nation, who may be cast upon their shores, and such has been the course of the Americans with respect to all Japanese subjects who have fallen under their protection.

The government of the United States desires to obtain from that of Japan some positive assurance that persons who may hereafter be shipwrecked on the coast of Japan, or driven by stress of weather into her ports, shall be treated with humanity.

…the President desires to live in peace and friendship with your imperial majesty, but no friendship can long exist, unless Japan ceases to act towards Americans as if they were her enemies.

> Letter drafted by Millard Fillmore, to be delivered to the Emperor of Japan through the commander of the mission, Commodore Matthew C. Perry.

Most contemporary historians who have researched the rationale behind Perry's mission to Japan have assumed that each of Fillmore's stated goals for the mission—friendship, commerce, coal and provisions, and protection for stranded crewmen—should be treated as mutually exclusive elements of a large, ambiguous whole designed to eventually secure commercial relations with Japan. This exclusivity treats the humanitarian thrust of the mission as separate from the mission's commercial goals. Such an assumption eventually leads to the determination that the whaler's stories of maltreatment were exploited by the Fillmore administration to justify the mission. Historian John Curtis Perry's conclusion about the waling community's lack of reaction to the Lawrence and Lagoda incidents typifies the results if this chain of logic if followed to its end:

> But although much talk was bruited about in Washington about the desirability of improving the situation of American whalers in the North Pacific by making Japanese ports havens for them, the whalers themselves did not lobby for such governmental assistance…Their plight seems simply to have provided additional ammunition to those interested in opening Japan for other reasons.[1]

However, one notices that this conclusion and others like it belie attempts by several individuals who strongly advocated that any mission to Japan include, at least as a component, assurances from the Japanese government that unfortunate castaways be treated according to common notions of kindness. These individuals are either notably absent from the discussion of the mission or they are unwittingly recruited as members of a plot to veil the commercial aspirations of the mission in a fog of humanitarian necessity.

Historian William L. Neumann, in his seminal work on U.S.-Japanese relations, *America Encounters Japan: From Perry to MacArthur*, published in 1963, identified himself as a strong proponent of the "commerce first" explanation; however, nine years earlier he had attempted to identify individuals who believed a mission to Japan was necessitated by humanitarian concerns. In an article printed in the *Pacific Historical Review* in 1954, Neumann admitted that commerce did not supply the only motivations for going to Japan, and that "for many Americans the Japan expedition was to serve far nobler ends."[2] He determined that, for many, "commerce and civilization were commonly believed to progress hand in hand," and in defense of using American gunboats to help spread that progress, Neumann believed "no inference of hypocrisy can be drawn against the claimants…[who] were expressing…a sincere belief in the magic touch of their nation."[3] If he, and other scholars who followed him, had chosen to examine those thoughts more carefully, the Perry mission might have been interpreted in such a way as to lend legitimacy to the altruistic aspects of the mission. Those "beliefs," if truly "sincere," represented the human desires of the hearts and minds of individuals who developed, planned, and implemented a mission that other naval powers, including earlier manifestations of the U.S. Navy, had attempted and failed.

How the Popular Case is Made

Historians, for the most part, have been singularly unsympathetic to the plight of the crews of the *Lawrence* and *Lagoda* after a cursory examination of their narratives. The sailors were incorrigible, unruly, and rude to each other and their Japanese captors. Some of the men attempted to escape time, and time, again, after being repeatedly warned not to. And, perhaps the most damning piece of evidence is that the crew of the *Lagoda* eventually confessed to being mutineers rather than unfortunate victims of their vessel's demise. Historically, three pieces of evidence have distracted, in hindsight, from the stories that the whalers of the *Lagoda* recounted. First, the behavior of the whalers toward their Japanese captors was far from congenial. Secondly, the crew of the Lagoda lied about the reasons for their being stranded. And, finally, supplemental testimony from an individual who was incarcerated concurrently demonstrated, at least upon selective reading, that the Japanese treated him with respect, thus negating the testimony of the whalers.

Japanese officials also sternly denied that they treated harshly the men of the *Lagoda* without just cause. In a memorandum addressed to the Dutch superintendent on Deshima, the local magistrate wrote:

> These men may complain about their treatment, but the landing of foreigners without permission is strictly forbidden by our laws, and yet these men were treated with kindness and informed about the stipulations of our laws. In spite of this, they repeatedly broke down their enclosures and fled, so that they might justly be severely

punished, but, with special clemency, they shall now be given up to the ship, as requested.[4]

Historians who discount the story of the *Lagoda* whalers often cite the narrative of Ranald MacDonald, an American who was in simultaneous captivity. On 27 June 1848, MacDonald purposely foundered a small boat near Japan for the express purpose of visiting the secluded nation without having to seek official admission.[5] After an initial imprisonment, MacDonald was transferred to Nagasaki, and finally repatriated to the *Preble* along with the *Lagoda* sailors. MacDonald immediately placed the onus of blame on the whalers:

> They were all young, violent, habitually quarreled amongst themselves, and gave much trouble….There was no "throat cutting," nor even corporal punishment, they were simply caged, and more closely guarded than the others. McCoy was one of the two. In fact, McCoy made a second or even third escape. He was then tied, and put into a sort of stocks….
>
> All this time, and throughout their whole detention—a period of twelve months—they were according to their own account, well and certainly not cruelly treated; as prisoners ever, however. No punishment was inflicted. One American died; a natural death, and notwithstanding all medical care and humane treatment; the only other death among them was that of a Sandwich Islander, who, in the manner of his people, without compunction, hung himself.[6]

After discounting the whalers' stories, historians' examinations easily follow a trail of influential businessmen, military officers, and politicians who all cited, at least in part, fiscal advantages to opening commercial relations with Japan. Businessmen such as Aaron Haight Palmer, interested in trade with all parts of Asia, spent countless hours and a sizeable sum of their own money to lobby government officials for a mission to Japan.[7] Palmer had penned numerous letters to politicians and businessmen, describing in detail the state of Japan (albeit somewhat naively) and the benefits of entering into a commercial partnership with Japanese merchants. This culminated in the dispatching of two letters to Secretary of State John

Clayton, the first of which stressed the commercial viability of trade with Asian nations and their aggregate populations of "over 140,000,000" future consumers for American goods. In his second letter, Palmer included a draft of a letter he had early written for President Zachary Taylor entitled "For the National Era: A Plan for Opening Japan," which was a multi-part plan that expressed the advantages of ports in Japan, along with the necessity to protect and foster whaling interests in the Pacific.

Another influential statesmen who lends partial legitimacy to "commerce first" adherents was Secretary of State Daniel Webster. It was he who drafted, on 10 June 1851, Commodore John H. Aulick's instructions for his abortive attempt to open Japan to diplomatic and commercial relations. [8] Surprisingly, Webster purposely chose to omit "all reference to the insults which had been offered to the American flag and the indignities and cruelties suffered by American citizens and officers in the...*Lagoda*, and other affairs."[9] Few speculate on why Webster chose to admit the mention of presumed Japanese indignities, but most point out that his instructions to Aulick was rife with mentions of coal, which was necessary to form "the last link in the chain of oceanic steam navigation."[10]

Matthew C. Perry himself often stated the non-humanitarian benefits of establishing, at a minimum, provisioning stations in Japan. Before he was given command of the East Asia Squadron, which eventually dropped anchor in Edo Bay, Perry was responsible for overseeing the construction of mail steamers and felt that fast mail delivery across the Pacific would "complete the circle of bi-monthly communications around the entire globe."[11] Perry was also acutely qualified to understand weaknesses of steamships, especially their interminable appetite for fuel, which necessitated the strategic positioning of coaling stations in order to keep a fleet of steam-powered vessels tenable.

A selective reading of the Democratic Party's opinion on the Perry's mission written in 1853 seemingly confirms that Whig politicians did, in fact, disguise a commercial mission in a façade of humanitarian necessity.

> [Whigs] shuffle, and make splendid flourishes about the "last link in the chain of civilization;" and, after assuring the Emperor of Japan that we shall invariably treat Japanese sailors who may be wrecked on our coasts with the greatest kindness (a safe enough undertaking), request as a favor, that his Imperial Highness will explain what he did with the American sailors who were wrecked on the coast of Japan some years ago. This is a poor sort of subterfuge.
>
> …we shall not be instrumental in disseminating throughout the country a pitiful story about murdered sailors, when it is obvious that it is a mere flimsy cloak to a matter-of-fact, business-like design.[12]

These sentiments, combined with detailed knowledge of the soon-undertaken and successful (for the U.S.) Townsend Harris commercial mission, provide ample, albeit circumstantial evidence furthering the legitimacy of the "commerce first" theory.

Reinterpreting the Historical Evidence

In total, evidence examined in such an order places both Whig politicians and the men of the *Lagoda* in a precarious position. However, the logic used to draw this conclusion relies on several assumptions. First, that one political party or group of influential individuals were stating their convictions with relative honesty, while their counterparts were presenting theirs with equal parcels of dishonesty. Secondly, that Whigs, were, as the *Democratic Review* stated, interested in commercial interests more than humanitarian, but were willing to feign concern for their fellow man in an attempt to simply pry open the closed door of Japan. Thirdly, that the testimony of the *Lagoda* mutineers should be discounted, because they were both prevaricators and unruly guests from the outset and they received treatment that they "deserved." If these assumptions can be set aside and the decisions leading to the Perry mission can be re-examined in a historical context not yet considered, the mission takes on a much different light.

What of the whalers? Yes, the men of the *Lagoda* were mutineers, but a careful examination of writings from both sides of the argument reveal that never does the fact that the whalers were mutineers directly impact the outcome of either party's experiences. The fabrication of their unfortunate circumstance as related to Japanese officials had been consistent with an attempt to gain as much sympathetic treatment as possible. Although some suspected that stories of the sailors' maltreatment were exaggerations, records of horrific tortures and executions, especially those directed at Christians, were known to have happened during the Tokugawa Era. Did not the whalers have justification to be cautious as they were undoubtedly familiar with tales of earlier encounters with the Japanese?[13] Also, most whalers who plied their trade off Hokkaido had certainly been exposed to stories of other unfortunates landing on those shores.[14] No matter what perceptions were, the men of the *Lagoda* had no choice but to survive the best they could and chose to represent themselves as members of the world's unfortunates. Unfortunately for them, many influential Japanese leaders assumed, all throughout Japan's period of isolation, that Western powers wanted nothing more than to subvert the Japanese government with Christianity and military might. This, in turn, affected the way in which officials viewed all Westerners, including the crews of cargo or whaling vessels. For historians to make simple whalers pay in retrospect for Japan's inability to cope with Westerners who were frightened and not of congenial manners or educated upbringing is too much to ask of them.

Although the men of the *Lagoda* were successful keeping from Japanese officials the fact that they were mutineers, it may have not mattered to many Japanese officials. The Japanese consistently harbored the belief that most castaways were spies sent to ascertain the military strength of Japan or to subvert its population with the heretical act of proselytizing for the Christian faith. Several Tokugawa-era scholars concluded that any requests for water or provisions were surely a precursor to an invasion and wrote extensively to the subject. Aizawa Seishisai, a Confucian scholar who studied the West extensively, developed a number of theses concerning how Japan should view and respond to Westerners. In 1824, Aizawa was dispatched to Otsuhama to assist in the interrogation of twelve English whalers who came ashore and promptly incarcerated. Aizawa spent five days interrogating the captain, who was one of the imprisoned sailors, and his crew. Mostly through non-verbal and non-written communication, Aizawa divined that the men were seeking to turn Japan into an English colony based on their drawing of the circuitous route from England to the island nation. When the captain drew a picture of a whale, indicating that was the reason for their presence near Japan, Aizawa dismissed it as an obvious "attempt to cover up the truth."[15] He further concluded that the captain was not simply the commander of a vessel, but part of an advanced scout team from the Kingdom of Great Britain. Additionally, Aizawa believed that all citizens of Western nations adhered to the "wicked doctrine of Jesus," and were thus connected to a larger subversive force, one that was already perceived as problematic to Japan's past.[16] He finally concluded that future requests for "water, provisions, and firewood to be a form of reconnaissance, the prelude to attack or subversion."[17]

What of Ranald MacDonald's testimony? Although he had high praise for the "common people" of Japan, who "appeared to be amiable and friendly," he still found fault in the government and its agents who were "in reverse."[18] Ranald McDonald testified to officers aboard the *Preble* that he was questioned at length about his religion. Furthermore, he testified that the response given to him upon his request for a Bible was "not to speak of the Bible in Japan; it was not a good book," thus confirming a substantial portion of the Whigs testimony and the whalers' stories about how people of Christian faith were treated in Japan. Additionally, MacDonald confirms some of the whalers' experiences, such as how he was confined below decks on his journey to Nagasaki:

> When the parties from the shore had left, I was put into a small cabin, grated: was, in fact, caged. There I remained all the rest of the voyage, with a pile of arms at my door, unable to see anything outside except on two or three occasions.
>
> I remonstrated against such close confinement, and on the following day the Captain ordered the removal of the grating, but I was told not to go on deck.[19]

Additionally, MacDonald had reason to believe that the whalers may have been doomed to a long incarceration in Japan:

> I was fully under the impression that the fifteen men…were still in Japan, and doomed to perpetual imprisonment; and that I believed that their liberation depended entirely upon the success of my efforts to return to civilization and send them relief.[20]

And, what of the Japanese magistrate's note? After his explanation as to why the whalers were treated harshly, he continued on to forbid whalers from hunting in "neighboring waters," Now, being duly warned, any further small craft, such as lifeboats and launches, were to land on Japanese shores, they would have certainly been sent for the express purpose of spying or sedition, since they would not be able to sail to Japan from the distances American ships were now instructed to stand:

> In the future, the laws of our country will be strictly enforced, should any men come in small boats and land without permission, even though they should claim shipwreck, for that would not be a case of a ship falling into dire want while passing at a great distance from Japan. It goes without saying that it is naturally difficult for small boats to cross wide seas, as in the case of the seven shipwrecked men of two years ago.[21]

> After all, [these cases of promiscuous landings arise because] boats go to and fro in seas near Japan. In future, these boats must never again come to fish in neighboring waters. Deliver these men to the captain of the American ship with this warning.[22]

The argument that New England merchants' failure to ask for protection proves that they did need or want it is a red herring. This logic is misleading and belies a simple fact: New England merchants and whalers did not ask for protection simply because they assumed they already had it. Although modern-day State Department officials are embroiled constantly in issues of treaties that guarantee or deny rights to our merchants, in the mid-nineteenth century, merchants relied on concepts of universal law and civility in order to maintain order. As the need for formal treaties grew along with the ever-increasing complexity of oceanic trade, commanders of fleets, such as Commodore Perry, were the official representatives of the State Department, charged as plenipotentiaries to deal with situations as they occurred. Thus, formal naval protection did not exist in the realm of codification; it relied on tradition and "common sense" notions of civility in which to operate.

A more accurate way to approach this problem is twofold. First, merchants had promoted several individuals such as Daniel Webster, who was a Massachusetts Whig, into government; therefore, their representation was already in place. Even unofficial merchant spokesmen such as Aaron Palmer "expressed his humanitarian concern, as well as his offended national pride, at the barbarous treatment afforded to shipwrecked American seamen in Japanese waters."[23] Secondly, the U.S. naval protection afforded to American merchants in the Pacific was an established tradition that began in 1832. At that time merchants in the East Indies had requested Andrew Jackson to provide a naval presence in the waters of the Indian and eastern Pacific Oceans. Before that time, Americans had been engaged in highly lucrative spice trade without major incident beginning immediately after the end of the Revolutionary War. However, in 1831, the capturing and subsequent looting by Sumatran forces of a Salem merchant ship, the *Friendship*, engaged in spice trade prompted the merchants request that an American man-of-war make a presence in the area. A year later, the first ship to be assigned to the East India Squadron (the same squadron commanded by Perry), the U.S.S. *Potomac*, carrying 282 officers and able seaman attacked, by land and sea, four forts on the Sumatran coast at the cost of 150 Sumatran lives and thirteen American casualties. In doing so, the United States was well within its rights, granted universally through Western understanding of universal laws to address the situation in Sumatra.

And what of Democratic claims that Whigs were less than sincere? In summer 1852, the *American Whig Review* upheld the party's belief that Perry's mission protected the lives of not only American sailors, but unfortunate Japanese seafarers who found themselves adrift and unable to return to Japan against the orders of the shogunate. The article offered several humanitarian justifications for undertaking the mission. First, was the lack of religious freedom illustrated by the punishments meted out to Christians after the Japanese government required to adherents of that faith to "abjure Christianity by insulting the figure of Christ and the Virgin, or be put to death."[24] The second was the Japanese government's failure to allow the people of Japan to allow "civilization" progress even "a year during a century." Third, the Japanese ignored the "rites of hospitality," even to the point that their own "sailors would not be apt to prefer going to the bottom of the sea rather than escape on a strange shore or a strange vessel." Fourthly, that Japan not only hindered the free choice of religion, but actually forced people to renounce their faith by "insulting the figure of Christ and the Virgin," on pain of being "put to death." Each one of these reasons correlated directly to the treatment of the recently incarcerated sailors or events experienced by relatively recent visitations to the islands by ships such as the *Morrison* and the *Manhattan*.

Addressing the plight of sailors directly, the article recounted the horrific stories circulating among the sailors, who regarded a "shipwreck on the coast of Niphon or of Saghalien as the most terrible disaster which could befall a mariner."[25] The article's specifics are worth quoting in full.

> The most facetious cruelty, it was said, was practiced upon any one who had been spared by the waves to the tender mercies of the Japan islander. His nose was amputated, and his ears cut close to his head. His alternate fingers were dexterously removed, and his feet were deprived of even the semblance of toes. Sometimes his cheeks were drilled, and sometimes his eyelids were sewed together. Mangled after one or another of these fashions, he was exhibited from town to town as a specimen of the physical education of foreigners, and as a warning to all beholders how they ever suffered themselves to contemplate the admission of such outlandish customs. What eventually became of these unfortunate witnesses to that "barbarian" system of decoration, which the Japanese of the inland so firmly believed, no one could say. It was sometimes hinted that they were made the subjects of cannibal appetite and the mildest form of death imagined for them was held to be torture, inflicted by some one of those ingenious methods for which, in cases of criminal punishments, the Japanese executioners are so deservedly remarkable.[26]

The author quickly conceded that nautical imagination was prone to exaggeration, but that it would have been "unjust to the Japanese to deny them the merit of these recherché cruelties altogether, however much they may have been magnified."[27]

Although these claims, on their own, could constitute a mere ploy, historians often ignore the influential Whigs who consistently mentioned humanitarian necessity in their writings concerning the mission. It is certainly important to understand the position of Palmer, Webster, and Perry, but what of men such as President Millard Fillmore and acting Secretary of State Charles M. Conrad? Both drafted the official instructions given to Perry and both were outspoken proponents of the humanitarian basis for the mission.

One of the least studied individuals to have a hand in the Perry mission is President Millard Fillmore. As both the Head of State and Government and the U.S. Commander-in-Chief, he was ultimately responsible for the undertaking of the mission. Perhaps it is not surprising that Fillmore receives negligible credit for the mission, given his poor reputation among both historians and non-historians alike. One recent biographer cited objective evidence demonstrating Fillmore's continued unpopularity.

> No president of the United States...has suffered as much ridicule as Millard Fillmore...Among...professors of American history or political science [who were polled in surveys]...he was in the Below Average or Worst Category. In the Murray-Blessing survey at Penn State, Fillmore ranked 25th of 36 presidents.[28]

Surprisingly, even shortly after his tenure as President ended, the fact that Fillmore helped launch the mission to Japan was nearly forgotten. W. L. Barre, Fillmore's hagiographer, completely neglects to mention it in his biography of the thirteenth President, written just a short time later in 1856.[29] So complete was the drift away from Fillmore that historian Tyler Dennett, in 1922, argued that historians were wrongly crediting Franklin Pierce's administration for the mission because "Neither Pierce nor [his Secretary of State William H. Marcy]...made any positive or constructive contribution to the task of opening the ports of

Japan."[30] Subsequent authors have given credit back to the Fillmore administration, but give very little credit to Fillmore himself.

Historians is recent years have sought to cast aside historical prejudices in order to re-examine Fillmore. In his 2001 study of the thirteenth President, historian Robert J. Scarry concluded that Fillmore "has been vastly underrated by historians who have not appraised him fairly," and attempted to remedy this by approaching the former President "with sympathy," treating him "as a much maligned and misunderstood individual who served at a critical time in our history."[31]

Almost half a century earlier, Robert Rayback came to a similar conclusion about Fillmore in his 1959 biography, writing

> When I began my research for this book, I expected to find that [he] was a weak and pompous president...instead, my investigation revealed that he possessed extra-ordinary strength of character and an enviable tenacity of purpose—as well as an admirable personality—I was startled.[32]

Asian Historian Harry Emerson Wildes was among the first historians to give Fillmore credit for his involvement in the Perry mission, writing in 1937 that he was "outspoken in his insistence that consideration of humanity required an opening of Japan's closed harbors."[33] Wildes' conclusion, although not popular with subsequent historians, is supported by the work of recent historical inquiry into Fillmore himself. Robert Rayback viewed Fillmore's foreign policy as one that "[promoted], by honorable means only, every legitimate interest of Americans. This meant that bellicose action or unwonted greed on the part of either foreigners or Americans must be restrained."[34] He asserted that Fillmore was "no worshiper of acquisitive Manifest Destiny," and pointed out that in the President's first annual presentation to Congress in December 1850, he stated his belief that American foreign policy should act towards other nations as we wish them to act towards us, and justice and conscience should form the rule of conduct between Governments, instead of mere power, self-interest, or the desires of aggrandizement. To maintain…friendly relations, to reciprocate every noble and generous act…these are the duties which we owe to other States, and by the performance of which we best entitle ourselves to like treatment from them; or if that, in any case, be refused, we can enforce our own rights with justice and a clear conscience."[35]

In historian Benson Lee Grayson's 1981 study of Fillmore's presidency, the author examined the foreign policy of the Fillmore administration and determined that the President's foreign policy was consistent with his beliefs as spoken in his 1850 presentation. Grayson believed that historians, caught in "in today's more cynical age," regarded Fillmore's words to "appear either hopelessly naïve or [to articulate] broad generalizations whose author scarcely intended to pursue them."[36] However, Grayson argued that "Fillmore took these principles seriously and proceeded to follow them."[37] Scarry concurred with Grayson's findings and found that Fillmore's "actions in foreign policy indicated the personal courage of his clear and unequivocal convictions instead of popularity and patriotism ahead of party."[38]

Some historians have accused Fillmore of allowing Secretary of State Daniel Webster to completely dictate his administration's foreign policy. A common belief that Fillmore was weak and unassertive man aids in this conclusion. In fact, Fillmore did, on several occasions, act as a foil to Webster's strident attitude and he proved to be a moderate voice on several foreign policy initiatives involving natural commodities of great importance to the United States. One example was Guano, a substance created from the droppings of seafowl and bats, was a necessary fertilizer, which could not be obtained in great quantities on the mainland United States. Peru, with an advantageous geographical and climatologically location, controlled a vast deposits of guano. U.S. merchants desired to harvest guano from the many islands located just outside of Peru's jurisdiction in an effort to avoid paying tariffs. U.S. merchants began to query Secretary of State Webster for U.S. naval protection in order to collect guano from these islands. Webster responded in the affirmative since the islands were technically outside of Peru's jurisdiction. Peru, however, had claimed the islands based on Pizarro's earlier discovery, and incessantly lobbied Webster to reverse his decision, but he did not. Peru, much like Japan, had little ability to defend itself, but informed Webster that it would do all within its power to secure the islands. Upon hearing of Webster's intentions, Fillmore reviewed Peru's position, and agreed that the islands were its possessions. Fillmore made it clear to Webster that he would not authorize the use of the U.S. navy to protect the merchants if they attempted to harvest the guano. Upon hearing that their support had been lost, the merchants, already in final preparations, abandoned their mission.[39]

In contrast to many historians' views that Webster was one of the primary arbitrators of foreign policy during the Fillmore administration, very little credit is given to his acting secretary of state, Charles Magill Conrad, who was responsible for finalizing and approving Perry's orders. Conrad, in general, is an understudied figure in American history. Only one biography of the former statesman is extant, and it does not address his role in the Perry mission. His previous decisions, however, may exhibit his attitudes toward the role of the government in promoting the humanitarian goals of the mission.

Conrad, a Democrat from the state of Louisiana was first elected to the U.S. Senate on March 10, 1842, by the state legislature as a replacement for the previous senator, who chose to run for Louisiana state governor. Immediately upon his arrival in Washington on April 14, 1842, Conrad was placed on the Committee on Military Affairs. Shortly thereafter, a bill came before the Senate seeking to refund a fine given to Andrew Jackson in 1815. Although he was an ardent Democrat, his "intensity of conviction" would not allow him to vote for the fine to be rescinded, because he felt that it was a reasonable and sound decision. [40] Historian William C. Honeycutt, Conrad's only biographer, viewed the politician as having a "meticulous sense of honesty" and a "tenacious loyalty to any cause which he espoused."[41]

Daniel Webster had initially directed Perry to write his own instructions for the mission. However, he did so during the final days of his life, which meant that the final official responsibility to write and approve the order was Conrad's. Historians are not able to determine how closely Conrad's signed orders deviated from Perry's self-written instructions, but the first priority for the mission, according to the finalized instructions was to "effect some permanent arrangement for the protection of American seamen and property wrecked [on Japan], or driven into their ports by stress of weather."[42] Honeycutt believed that Conrad approached problems with "businesslike methods" and "refused to become excited or to allow the passions of the day to cause him to swerve from his conception of duty."[43] Conrad did not always agree with Fillmore, "but had always considered him honest," and the two men agreed on the issue of the whalers because Conrad "was always an earnest advocate of strict adherence, on the part of the government, to any agreement, expressed or implied."[44]

Fillmore himself proved that he was a President who was willing to become personally involved in international policy matters, but he was unwilling to promote armed conflict simply for the sake of business. On several occasions he was unwilling to authorize force unless a situation called for it, but through non-violent means managed to protect American rights anyhow. For example, in 1842, a Mexican named Don Jose de Garay obtained the rights from his government to build a railroad or canal across the Isthmus of Tehuantepec.[45] The rights were sold and bought several times until they finally came into the hands of American Peter A Hargous, who convinced several New Orleans businessmen to invest in the cross-isthmus railroad. Although it was Taylor's administration that laid the foundations for the business venture, little came of it. After Fillmore took office, the businessmen began pressing his administration for satisfactory results. Not willing to let matters simply rest with Fillmore, the businessmen informed the Mexican government that they would begin to lobby for military intervention if their rights were not upheld. Fillmore, true to his character, had no desire to employ the military to aid scored businessmen, and offered to re-negotiate the railroad rights on behalf of the investors. The resultant Treaty of Tehuantepec was ratified by the Senate and signed by Fillmore on February 25, 1851, but the Mexican government rejected it "due to pressure by the Catholic church, which feared American influence in Mexico."[46] The Mexican government relied on a clause in the original contract which stipulated that the construction of the railroad had to begin by July 1846, blatantly ignoring multiple extensions granted by former president Antonio Lopez de Santa Anna and then later Jose Mariano de Salas.

The situation deteriorated greatly soon after when, against treaty stipulations, the Mexican government forcibly halted the engineers, who had been sent with U.S. governmental guarantees of protection, from working on the railroad. Immediately, the investors petitioned Fillmore personally in Washington D.C. for a military intervention to enforce the treaty and to protect the American engineers. They had already decided that if Fillmore refused to send American troops, they would send their own personal army of 550 men to protect their men and keep them working. The investors knew all-too-well that the Mexican government would attempt to forcibly detain these men, who, according to the treaty, would have been there legally for the protection of the engineers and laborers. Consequentially, the United States would have no choice but to intervene militarily on behalf engineers, laborers, and the men sent to protect them. Not only had the Mexican government reneged on two important commercial treaties, but they were placing under duress the Americans who Millard Fillmore had personally promised to protect. Fillmore wrote to Secretary of State Webster and explained that he had plainly informed the investors that he was prepared to do anything he personally could do honorably to sustain the company, but was not willing to go to war with Mexico to "gratify…the cupidity of any private company."[47] Fillmore eventually secured U.S. rights for the railroad by appealing directly to Mexican President Arista and instructing the State Department to negotiate, through Mexican consul Alfred Conkling, a treaty which assured that the Mexican government would protect the railroad venture, even if that meant enlisting the help of the United States military.

Fillmore had a direct influence on Perry and his mission, for as the date for the Japan expedition neared, Perry and Fillmore had a relatively close and cordial relationship. Samuel Elliot Morrison's biography of Perry indicates that they met for the first time in May 1851 to celebrate new construction on the Hudson and Lake Erie Railroad. There, Fillmore "made a favorable impression on the Commodore, and it may be assumed that the feeling was mutual."[48] Their relationship grew closer as the start of the mission approach, and during Perry's stay in Washington prior to his departure, Fillmore dined with Commodore Perry on a regular basis while Perry was in Washington.[49] When the Commodore departed, Fillmore, along with his cabinet, went to bid him farewell aboard the Mississippi.[50] Perry revealed to his

wife, Jane, his appreciation for the president's support, saying that his power and authority "far

exceeded any that have hitherto been issued to any one—I only hope that I may be found equal

to the trust they have confided in me."[51]

Conclusion

The "commerce first" explanation for the Perry mission has done much to promote the

study of early U.S.-Japan relations. However, the theory has become so entrenched, that few

have proposed alternative interpretations. Few, if any, individuals at the time wrote only of the

commercial benefits of a possible Japan mission. Even Palmer, who wrote and lobbied

zealously on the economic benefits of opening Japan to trade, also promoted a mission on the

basis of humanitarian necessity. Additionally, "commerce first's" dominant position spotlights

individuals who seemingly chose to address the mission's commercial possibilities at the

expense of those who, at the very least, directed the mission with both commercial and

humanitarian goals in mind. If commercial interests were such an overwhelmingly dominant

force amongst politicians, businessmen, and the military elite who wanted to send a mission to

Japan, who, then, exactly needed to be fooled into believing that the mission was related to

humanitarian concerns at all?

The "commerce first" explanation also effectively dehumanizes the American attempt

to negotiate a treaty with Japan. Commerce implies greed, which, in turn, tends to demonize

the entire mission and its goals. One of the reasons for this may coincide with current

cynicism surrounding government actions. In essence, Japan was the underdog, and those

historians who dedicated great amounts of time to understanding and sympathizing with such a "foreign" nation could clearly see that they had no hope of evading the grasp of Western mercantile powers. Without the means to create modern weapons or to field a diplomatic corps capable of lobbying foreign governments on their behalf, Japan was apparently left with little recourse but to accept the Fillmore administration's demands. If viewed in this context, those historians may have developed a strong sense of *noblesse oblige* to advocate, in retrospect, on Japan's behalf. Caught in the center, as they had been in 1851, the crews of the *Lawrence* and *Lagoda* become pawns who were unwittingly placed in the forefront of Western policies assumed to be based on deceit and motivated by greed.

Finally, although the Perry mission to Japan was a momentous historical event, the tendency of historians interested in Japan or U.S.-Japan diplomatic relations is to overemphasize its significance within the greater context of U.S. maritime history. Much of the credit for the actual execution of the mission itself should be given to Perry, who spared no expense in the purchase of tribute gifts for the Japanese officials and who made it a point to demonstrate an extraordinary sampling of American culture and technological prowess. In contrast, the mission's original commander, John Aulick, planned to approach Japan without gifts or cultural demonstrations, which was much more in accord with standard diplomatic procedure at the time in the Far East beginning with the punitive mission of the U.S.S. *Potomac* in 1832. In essence, taking the Perry mission out of the greater context of maritime history enforces the idea that the mission was somehow extraordinary, and therefore, was driven by events too great to include the plights of common whalers. This rendition of history detracts from an obvious truth: that in the minds of many people at the time, humanitarian concerns, coupled with maritime legal precedents, were wholly justifiable reasons on their own for the Perry mission.

NOTES FOR CHAPTER III

1. John Curtis Perry, *Facing West: Americans and the Opening of the Pacific* (Westport, Conn.: Praeger, 1994), 83. Perry is a staunch advocate of the "commerce first" undertaking of the mission provides a comprehensive analysis of Perry's commercial aspirations for Japan and the rest of the Pacific.

2. William L. Neumann, "Religion, Morality, and Freedom: The Ideological Background of the Perry Expedition," *Pacific Historical Review* 28, no. 3 (1954): 248.

3. Ibid.

4. Reprinted in Sakamaki, 18.

5. Ranald MacDonald, was born in 1824 at Fort George, located within the present-day city of Astoria, Oregon. MacDonald spent much of his incarceration in Japan teaching officials English—many of his students negotiated with Westerners. In 1987, the Rishiri Rotary Club dedicated a monument at the point of MacDonald's initial landing in Notsuka, Japan. It was built to mark the "first spontaneous cultural exchange between Japan and North America." MacDonald died in 1894, his final utterance, "Sayonara." A monument has been erected at his birthplace in Astoria. For more information, see Jo Ann Roe, *Ranald MacDonald: Pacific Rim Adventurer* (Pullman: Washington State University Press, 1997) and an annotated reprint of his original manuscript (not published until 1923) by William S. Lewis and Naojiro Murakami, *Ranald MacDonald: The Narrative of His Early Life on the Columbia Under the Hudson's Bay Company's Regime; of His Experiences in the Pacific Whale Fishery; and of His Great Adventure to Japan'; With a Sketch of His Later Life on the Western Frontier, 1824-1894* (Portland: Oregon Historical Society Press, 1990). Since the original manuscript was not published until 1923, officials presiding over the Perry mission could only know of the testimony he gave to Lt. Cmdr. Glynn after his departure from Nagasaki.

6. Reprinted from his original manuscript in Lewis and Murakami, 197.

7. Aaron Haight Palmer is often cited in detail by historians, and is considered the quintessential businessman associated with the mission to Japan. His letters were reprinted, in detail, in the congressional records used to help sway votes in favor of the mission.

Additionally, Palmer printed, at his own expense, over 2,250 copies of his own memorandums for distribution to various government officials. Eventually, Palmer was directed to compile primary documents related to the mission, which was finally published in 1857 in Aaron Haight Palmer, *Documents and Facts Illustrating the Origin of the Mission to Japan* (Washington: Henry Polkhorn, 1857).

8. John H. Aulick, who was initially selected to lead the mission to Japan was able to gain his post, in part, thanks to Japanese castaways. On 1 March 1851, seventeen sailors of the ill-fated *Eiriki-Maru* were brought to San Francisco by the bark *Auckland*. Upon their arrival, Aulick wrote to Secretary of State Daniel Webster and argued that their repatriation may be precursor to further commercial negotiations. In fact, several attempts to repatriate Japanese castaways had ended with mixed results. An expulsion edict, issued n 1825, gave orders to fire upon unauthorized ships attempting to land on Japan was executed in 1837 when the brig *Morrison* arrived in Japan to repatriate seven Japanese castaways and were driven off by cannon fire during several attempts. Many other attempts were made to repatriate Japanese castaways, some successful, some not, but all labored under the pall of the unknown and the belief that the Japanese men would face punishment or even death upon their return. See Sakamaki, 12-29, 72-86, and passim; Robert Erwin Johnson, *Far China Station: The U.S. Navy in Asian Waters, 1800-1898* (Annapolis: Naval Institute Press, 1979), 50-51; and Katherine Plummer, *The Shogun's Reluctant Ambassadors: Japanese Sea Drifters in the North Pacific* (Portland: Oregon Historical Society Press, 1991), 6-8 and passim.

9. Denett, 261.

10. See Peter Booth Wiley and Korogi Ichiro, *Yankees in the Land of the Gods: Commodore Petty and the Opening of Japan* (New York: Viking, 1990), 100.

11. John Curtis Perry, 82-84,

12. "The Japan Expedition and its Results," *The United States Democratic Review* 32, no 1 (1853): 66-7.

13. See Introduction.

14. "Japan—the Expedition," *The American Whig Review* 15, no. 90 (1852): 508.

15. Wakabayashi, 88.

16. Ibid., 90.

17. Ibid.

18. *Imprisoned American Seamen,* 27.

19. Lewis and Murakami, 203.

20. Roe, 106.

21. This was in reference to the men of the *Lawrence,* who refused to cast off in their small boats because they were not made to be used in open sea.

22. Reprinted Sakamaki, 58-59.

23. Borst, 150.

24. "Japan—the Expedition," 508.

25. Ibid.

26. Ibid.

27. Ibid.

28. Robert J. Scarry, *Millard Fillmore* (Jefferson, N.C.: McFarland, 2001), 341-343.

29. W. L. Barre, *The Life and Public Services of Millard Fillmore* (Buffalo: Wanzer, McKim, and Co., 1856).

30. Dennett, 292-3.

31. Scarry, 2-3.

32. Robert J. Rayback, *Millard Fillmore: Biography of a President* (Buffalo: Buffalo Historical Society, 1959), vii.

33. Harry Emerson Wildes, *Aliens in the East: A New History of Japan's Foreign Intercourse* (Philadelphia: University of Pennsylvania Press, 1937), 242.

34. Rayback, 301.

35. Ibid., 318.

36. Benson Lee Grayson, *The Unknown President: The Administration of President Millard Fillmore* (Washington: University Press of American, 1981), 81.

37. Ibid.

38. Scarry, 215.

39. See Rayback, 318-20 and Scarry, 207-8.

40. William C. Honeycutt, "The Early Political Career of Charles Magill Conrad" (M.A. thesis, The Louisiana State University and A&M College, 1939), 27, 105.

41. Ibid.

42. Perry's instructions can be found in *Correspondence Relative to the Naval Expedition to Japan*, 2-11.

43. Honeycutt, 95.

44. Ibid., 88, 95.

45. See Scarry, 206-7; Rayback 307-9.

46. Scarry, 206.

47. Rayback, 308.

48. Samuel Elliot Morison, *"Old Bruin": The Life of Commodore Matthew C. Perry, 1794-1858* (Boston: Little, Brown and Company, 1967), 273.

49. Scarry, 213. Perry began his stay in January 1852, and he remained there until the start of mission.

50. John H. Schroeder, *Matthew Calbraith Perry: Antebellum Sailor and Diplomat* (Annapolis: Naval Institute Press, 2001), 183.

51. Schroeder, *Matthew Calbraith Perry,* quoted 183: From MCP to Jane Perry, 24 November 1852, Perry Papers, Harvard University.

CHAPTER IV

HUMANITARIANISM AND NATURAL LAW

IN THE NINETEENTH-CENTURY AMERICAN WORLDVIEW

Several historians have recently begun to examine how religious, ethical, and moral movements in the United States combined to shape the American worldview during the antebellum period. An understanding of this worldview is an important foundation from which to interpret the Perry mission. For antebellum Americans, whether Northern or Southern, Democrat or Whig, farmer or maritime merchant, commercial interests and humanitarian needs were considered by many, including the majority of policymakers, to go hand in hand. The prevailing rationale for this was that divine providence was the keystone to any endeavor, and only those who attempted to advance commerce for the good of all mankind would receive it.

In the antebellum political realm, both Democrats and Whigs based their primary considerations for going to Japan on the same set of moral codes. The common code of conduct influencing decision-makers in the nineteenth century rested on two foundations: moral culture and legal culture. Moral culture is more abstract and difficult to define than the legal culture, because in order to interpret it, one must interpret mass cultural movements in existence at the time and use them as a lens through which to view the individuals who were making prominent political decisions, such as Fillmore and Perry. Legal culture is somewhat easier to define, given that politicians, military officers, and businessmen interested in international trade were all required (albeit with varying degrees) to adhere to structures that had been formalized through tradition, laws, and treaties. This legal culture can be discerned in Western notions of what was then known as *natural law* (otherwise known as the law of nations, moral law, universal law, international law or by the term recently coined, international political theory).

Moral Culture and Northern Antebellum Religious Influences

Perhaps it is not surprising that historical inquiry into this period of Japanese and American relations tends to separate religion from commercial interests. Until only recently, historians have viewed antebellum and post-antebellum religion at the individual and communal levels (especially in the North) as distinctly separate from individual and communal political views. This is in stark contrast to the research done on colonial-era Northerners, who have been viewed as a group holding a "unified theory of power,"[1] which historian Mary Beth Norton defined as the belief that "all secular authority systems…[rested] on the same fundamental base."[2] This "base" centered on hierarchical relationships between the head of the household (which usually meant a father, but could also mean a widowed woman, as well), his family, and the government that he was both ruled by and empowered through his direct actions. However, at the power given to the actors in these relationships "was ordained by God," all participants "were inextricably linked to religious belief as well."[3]

While historians interested in the Antebellum southeastern United States freely discussed the religious and societal linkages to antebellum Southern culture, decidedly fewer have attempted similarly create these links in Northern culture—particularly Northern Protestant influences on economic policy. Historian Mark Noll opined that scholarship that could illuminate the connections between American Protestantism and the economics of the time has been absent because the politico-religious linkages were extraordinarily complex and those relationships were "a combination of unexplored factual questions and profoundly complicated structural connections."[4] Noll concluded that "Protestantism between the two wars of the United States' early existence must be regarded as a mountain where exploration has reached only to the foothills."[5] Additionally, he opined that "modern historians, some of whom, perhaps" are still cynical about human motivation, "find it difficult to take religion seriously as a primary motive for human action or to believe that religious speech can be anything but a screen for social or economic motives."[6]

Noll noted that many of the historical actors who were responsible for commercial policy during the antebellum era "did not sense the moral standoffs" perceived by modern historians who place their primary emphasis on "the history and character of market transformations."[7] Noll recommended viewing antebellum commercial society from a vantage point that treats "religion as a motivating factor, as well as a reacting factor."[8] If viewed in this manner, linkages between "communities, subsistence, production for local use, humane values, and religion as self-expression" and "individuals, profit, production for market exchange, commercial values, and religion as self-control" may appear less contradictory and more holistic in nature.[9]

In general, post-colonial Protestants belonged to either one of two groups. The first, "antiformalists," were generally from Baptist, Reformationalist, or early forms of Methodism that stressed charismatic worship, simple living, and an emotional connection to God.[10] This type of religious expression was generally concentrated in the South and its adherents were attracted to the Democratic Party. Members aligned with the other division, or "formalists," were generally from the ranks of the middle and upper classes, tended to be attracted to churches with more orderly and stoic forms of worship such as those offered by Congregational, Presbyterian and Episcopalian denominations (and latter forms of Methodism) and were the standard-bearers for Victorian decorum. These people tended to be Northerners who were commonly attracted to the Whig Party.[11]

There is another important distinction to make between the religious messages that drew Southerners and Northerners to their respective denominations. Antiformalists, in general, were attracted to various interpretations of John Calvin's teachings on salvation—that man was inexorably corrupt and only God could determine the fate of the saved and the damned. Formalists, on the other hand, were primarily followers of Jacobus Arminius' belief that man, through repentance and personal responsibility, could overcome original sin through his own efforts, and thus could be accepted by God through His grace. Because of this inherent belief in man's ability to affect the world around him, formalists were working under a "sense of human capacity and moral responsibility" that gave rise to a socio-religious ideal that "manifestly…affirmed a greater measure of human dignity" than the ideals of their antiformalist counterparts.[12] Thus, Whigs, by their very nature tended to believe "that every person had the potential to become moral and good" if placed in an environment that "nurtured the seed of goodness in his moral nature."[13]

Historian Daniel Walker Howe argued that the Arminian influence on religious expression allowed Americans to join a denomination or faith on a voluntary basis, which was, until that time, a "distinctly American phenomenon" that "was unique in the world."[14] Howe argued that, because worshippers were allowed to come to faith on their own terms and not those dictated to them by a government or monarch. This element of choice constituted for him or her a voluntary "service in the army of Christ, just as they volunteered for service in fire brigades, the militia,…labor unions, sewing circles, political parties, or Washingtonians."[15] However, unlike sewing circles, "most of the kinds of religion embraced by the antebellum Americans required some form of self-discipline," which, in turn, forced people to seek out like-minded companions who would help them stay their course. This type of interaction eventually "provided most of the impulse toward social organization."[16] Howe believed that it is these social organizations that drove its members toward Christian perfectionism, which spawned public outgrowths such as the temperance movement.

Christian perfectionism had one side-effect of great importance to the formation of the Perry mission—the concept of "polite culture," which was a result of religious volunteerism and the emergence of a middle-class consumer culture in the early nineteenth century. Howe contended that polite culture was an outgrowth of a "much larger trend toward the reformation of manners that was by no means simply religious."[17] Public and private manners were important because, unlike in the past when businessmen would communicate directly with their peers, the growing American commercial culture facilitated direct contact between merchants, businessmen, and middle-class consumers—individuals who were outside of each other's family or community's direct sphere of influence. Thus, middle-class politeness "was a giant undertaking of voluntary self-reconstruction made possible by the market revolution" and, if cultivated properly, demonstrated that an individual possessed "cultivation and good taste."[18]

Historian Ann C. Rose's recent study of American religious trends from 1830 to 1860 linked capitalism with the unified theory of power described by Norton, and determined that prevailing religious attitudes allowed a "capitalist mind-set" or a "culture of capitalism" to amalgamate into a new system of "values [that] spoke eloquently of this generation's powerful ambitious anxieties," which were "based on a faith that words and images, if carefully chosen and ordered as ideology, could bring tranquility of mind and peace in social relations"[19] From 1830 to 1850, Americans were so obsessed with the ramifications of polite culture that hundreds of etiquette manuals were published to feed their insatiable appetite for correctness.[20] By the time the stories of the *Lawrence* and *Lagoda* were read by Americans, "polite culture and evangelical religion" had combined to drive an "impulse to improve the individual and the world" and "to make the world a better place by reshaping individuals into better people."[21] On the greater world stage, politeness and the religious milieu surrounding it "was linked with the rise of humanitarianism," which "helped reshape the world into a place where violent behavior was discouraged and commercial relations between strangers would be facilitated."[22]

International Law and its Links to Humanitarianism

While an analysis of the American Victorian-era rise in humanitarian interest might help historians better understand why mercantilism alone did not account for America's interest in Japan, it does not specifically explain the creation of specific treaty articles to protect shipwrecked whalers. For this, one must analyze the pervading legal consciousness of the men who promoted the Perry mission. Although many historical interpretations of the mission discuss natural law as a talking point for those justifying the missions, the singular focus on commercial motivations has done little to define what natural law was and how it was defined, obscuring the traditional legal linkages to what was then (and is now) a fundamental component of maritime policy.

"Commerce first" theorists are not the first to omit traditional interpretations of natural law from their analyses, as the study of the concept as a whole has declined greatly in the twentieth century. There are several reasons for these omissions; first, modern law, as studied in the latter-half of the twentieth century, is based on an emotive theory of ethics, which presumes that "evaluational terms as ought, right, and good at not cognitive terms…they are merely the expression of biases and preferences." In other words, "like poetry, moral judgments use language in a nonrational, emotive way…"[23] This is in stark contrast to pre-twentieth century interpretations of natural law, which presumed that an outside force imposed a particular order on the universe and all things animate and inanimate. Thus, natural law, as it relates to mankind, eschewed emotive reasoning, and based the creation of laws on an accepted theories and philosophies that encouraged a "universal pattern of action, applicable to all…everywhere, required by human nature itself for its completion."[24]

The First World War drastically changed how the study of international law was approached as scholars of law and philosophy all tried to cope with the physical, social, and political detritus of the "War to End all Wars" and its worldwide legal outgrowth, the League of Nations. Although a great deal of emphasis was placed on the study of natural law as it related to the devastating events of the war, little emphasis was placed on its history.

In 1953, Harvard Professor of Philosophy John Wild noted that only "recently" had the study of the history of natural law been "revived, after a century and a half of neglect."[25] The machinery of this revival turned slowly. In 2002, Cambridge University Press published a primer on the ancient texts of natural law in order to support a "recent…revival of interest in the classical theory of international relations, or… 'international political theory.'"[26] The authors surmised that this renewal came about "because…there have been many periods in the past when the idea of a clear-cut distinction between the 'international' and the 'domestic' had not existed."[27] The years delineated by Wild and the "reintroduction" of the ancient texts relating to natural law demonstrate that the study of natural law was at its nadir during a period of great historical inquiry into the Perry mission. Thus, the absence of discussion of natural law as it related to Japanese-American relations in the mid-nineteenth century could simply be a matter of scholarship falling within a time frame when international political theory had given way to interpretations of "modern" law and its mutually distinct notions of international and domestic political realms.

Natural Law Defined

What appears odd at first glance in a modern context is the Whig concern that Japan had "blocked the rest of the world wholly out from any intercourse with themselves, and have grown gray in national stupefaction…in fact, the Japanese hardly go forward a year during a century."[28]As strange as this statement may sound if examined from a nineteenth-century standard, it is consistent with the mores and values held by many prominent politicians and business leaders.

As stated previously, natural law presumes that the world is in an ordered state; therefore, any actions, including the creation of law, must stay true to this natural order for humans to progress in a right manner. Natural law also assumes that the universe and each species within it have natural tendencies, the foremost of which is the tendency to live. John

Wild's succinct definition of natural law and its fundamental relationship to these tendencies, deserves to be quoted in length:

> What is meant by a natural tendency? This is marked by two distinguishing features: first, it is shared in common to all members of the species; second, its realizations, at least to some degree, is required for the living of human life. Thus, the need for food is a natural tendency; the desire to torture other men is not. The first is common to the species, and some degree of realization is required for human life. Hence, it is essential. The second lacks these marks. It is not common to the species. Human life can be achieved without it, and closer examination will reveal that it is an impediment to co-operative modes of action which are essential to human life. Hence, it is unessential or accidental, and also obstructive or evil.
>
> The pattern of action which is universally required for the living of human life is essential. This is the standard of natural law. All other acts are incidental. If they conflict with essential natural needs, they are evil. If they further the realization of such natural needs in the concrete, they are good. If they do neither, they are indifferent. This is the theory.[29]

This explanation for natural law has remained nearly unchanged since its definition in ancient Greece, but what has changed is the discussion of just what constitutes "human nature," and how that nature is governed.

The Historical Context for Natural Law

Inquiries into the formation of natural law often begin with its promulgation in the Roman state. However, the concept of natural law must begin with the Greeks, who are credited with the foundations of the modern state and the correlating idea that men were the primary individual component of the Greek's basic polity, the city-state. Plato envisioned the city-state as the final manifestation of mankind's attempt to rule themselves; therefore, the city-state, as a part of a larger society, would have to rule itself ethically and would be superior to a society ruled by a monarch. Men were thus the primary executors of the righteousness of the State as the whole and the combined authority of righteous men would eclipse that of even the most righteous autocratic ruler.

The law was what the Greeks "recognized as their sovereign in the state" and that law operated from "'a complex of ethical rules' based firmly upon fundamental and universally recognized principles of morality."[30] The righteous execution of law, in turn, "was a means of applying these principles to the multitudinous relations of human beings dwelling together in a society for the sake of 'the good life.'"[31] This ideal was confirmed in the minds of the Greeks after their victory over the Persians, as the latter was ruled by an autocratic sovereign. The victory also imbued the Greeks with a new-found sense of civilization; the strength they found through combined polity was superior to all others. From that point on, this type of self-assurance made the Greeks promote common interests above individual rights.

Zeno and the Stoics

What the Platonic ideal of the city-state did not account for, however, was how law based on "reason" should be applied to foreign civilizations. It was the Greek philosopher Zeno who, having grown up in a Hellenic trading city, understood that the harmonious intermingling of Greeks and non-Greeks would have to take into account more than the Platonic notions of their own society and the inner workings of their own city-state system. The school of thought he founded, Stoicism, attempted to apply "reason" to those living outside Greece and eventually concluded that all men had the power to choose to practice that which was "reasonable" and that which was "unreasonable," since "reason" as a concept had to transcend the notions of nation and society, Greek and non-Greek, and East and West. Therefore, Stoics concluded that reason must be "divine and all-pervading."[32] Zeno argued that since reason was based on divine principles and all things on Earth, were imbued with it, "'the world is a product of reason, and…all the laws of nature aim in the long run at reasonable ends.'" Zeno and Stoics thus provided for the primary expansion of natural law beyond its foundations in the city-state, because "reason here becomes identified on the one hand with a universal mind or soul, and on the other with a universal ruling principle, or law."[33]

Historian James Brown Scott summarized the Stoic belief system when he wrote that the Stoics "believed that all things were subject to 'universal order,' which is arranged by, or rather is conceived as being, a supreme and all-pervading intelligence."[34] This summary, however, does not provide for an ultimate purpose for the law or for man. Scott also noted that Stoics further determined that nature was evolving, in a divine manner, in such a way that every living thing was becoming more perfect. This is not to be confused with Darwinian evolution, for the term in the Stoic sense refers to "growth" or "the process of growth" mandated by nature and which was controlled by the divine—all things grow to fulfill their function according to divine purpose.[35]

How, then, did humans fit into this divine purpose? Although one may not know his ultimate purpose, only those that are truly free will be able to fulfill their divinely manifested destiny.[36] The Stoic interpretation of natural law required that all must have equal access to this freedom, and therefore "under the universal law he is on an equal plane of equality with all other men…since he is a reasoning creature, he is individually responsible for his own development."[37] Therefore, "man stands alone and the Stoic is an individualist," while at the same time "he is also part, with all other human beings of nature."[38] In the latter sense, all men were citizens of the world. If this Stoic interpretation of natural law were to be enacted on a worldwide basis, people should eventually consider themselves part of one worldwide community, but only the freedom to continually evolve would eventually allow mankind to eventually reach this goal.

The Development of Maritime Law

As the Romans conquered and consolidated neighboring states into their empire, their statesmen had to implement policy that would allow the conquered nations to retain as much of their own law as possible, while maintaining a distinct, but standardized set of laws necessary to govern trade over the disparate empire. It was Zeno's interpretations of natural law that found a receptive audience with the Roman lawmakers and philosophers charged to solve this dilemma. Romans were accustomed to adapting and changing many elements of Greek culture to suit their needs, and natural law was no exception.

It is from Roman trade laws that maritime law developed, and all "civilized" nations within the empire adhered to them. After the fall of the Roman Empire, however, commercial relations, especially those of a maritime nature, did not cease to exist. The one unifying force during the Middle Ages was the Roman Catholic Church, which became the *de facto* arbiter of international disputes as it was one of the only organizations with the power, influence, and reach necessary to negotiate with "heathen" nations that were beyond the military influence of European states. Rarely did the Church have to contend with countries within its sphere of influence, because the codes of maritime conduct within the Roman Empire had become remarkably uniform and universally acknowledged by that time.[39]

Nations outside of the auspices of the Roman Catholic Church ("heathens") were a different matter, as they had no tradition of maritime codes based on Stoic ideas of natural law.

It was not uncommon for nations outside of the realm to claim "Right of Wreck" by drawing trading vessels close to their jagged shores, plundering the ships as they broke up, and selling their take for profit and the crew into slavery. In an effort to apply a universal standard to these and other maritime incidents, bishops and papal commissions began to codify maritime customs, as they were called, to settle these types of disputes.

The historical beginnings of a canonical maritime law is often credited to Eleanor (1121-1204), heir to the wealthy province of Aquitaine (now part of modern France) and the island of Oleron. While participating in an ill-fated crusade to the Holy Land, she learned of the maritime conventions that the Mediterranean countries she passed through used to maintain order. After her return, she codified these conventions and promulgated them to Aquitaine and Oleron from 1152 to 1160. These conventions became Europe's first "admiralty," or maritime laws known by various names, including the "Rolls of Oleron," the "Laws of Oleron," and the "Rules of Oleron."

Relevant to the discussion of shipwrecked sailors was "article," or "judgment," twenty-nine, which stated, in full:

> If any ship or other vessel sailing to and fro, and coasting the seas, as well in the way of merchandizing, as upon the fishing account, happen by some misfortune through the violence of the weather to strike herself against the rocks, whereby she becomes so bruised and broken, that there she perishes, upon what coasts, country or dominion soever; and the master, mariners, merchant or merchants, or any one of these escape and come safe to land; in this case the lord of that place or country, where such misfortune shall happen, ought not to let, hinder, or oppose such as have so escaped, or such to whom the said ship or vessel, and her lading belong, in using their utmost endeavors for the preservation of as much thereof as may possibly be saved. But on the contrary, the lord of that place or country, by his own interest, and by those under his power and jurisdiction, ought to be aiding and assisting to the said distressed merchants or mariners, in saving their shipwrecked goods, and that without the least embezzlement, or taking any part thereof from the right owners; but, however, there may be a remuneration or consideration for salvage to such as take pains therein,

according to right reason, a good conscience, and as justice shall appoint; notwithstanding what promises may in that case have been made to the salvors by such distressed merchants and mariners, as is declared in the fourth article of these laws; and in case any shall act contrary hereunto, or take any part of the said goods from the said poor, distressed, ruined, undone, shipwrecked persons, against their wills, and without their consent, they shall be declared to be excommunicated by the church, and ought to receive the punishment of thieves; except speedy restitution be made by them: nor is there any custom or statute whatsoever, that can protect them against the aforesaid penalties, as is said in the XXVI article of these laws.[40]

Early versions of the article added that those who failed to abide by this humanitarian

standard were

contrary to the commandment of God Omnipotent, notwithstanding any custom or ordinance, it is said and *decreed* that the lord, the salvors and the others who shall take anything of the said goods, shall be accursed and excommunicated and punished as robbers.[41]

American Interpretations of Natural Law

The formation of the American state was partly influence by the European Renaissance and its emphasis on Classical Republicanism, which rejected monarchism and carried with it a "strong conviction that nature has a purpose."[42] When these ideals were combined with Enlightenment thinking, which stated that governments should be balanced and orderly, men once again were encouraged to expand on the notion of natural law in both the context of the divine and its relationship to nature. The interpretation of natural law in Emmerich de Vattel's *The Law of Nations or the Principles of Natural Law Applied to the Conduct and the Affairs of Nations and of Sovereigns* (1758) struck a balance between the two, thereby becoming "unrivaled among such treatises in its influence on the American founders,"[43] and therefore the development of American foreign policy. Natural law historian James Brown Scott concluded that "Vattel's statement of [natural] law has been for more than a century looked upon by the Supreme

Court…as an authoritative statement."[44] Why, then, was Vattel's interpretation of natural law

so prominent in the development of the American state?

Vattel's work, unlike many that came before it, was both contemporary (since it was

published in 1758) and concerned with "both internal as well as foreign affairs,"[45] which was

welcomed by a new nation seeking to define itself both domestically and internationally.

Vattel's interpretation of natural law also presumed that nations were independent of one

another, and therefore could enact their own laws (a primary justification for the

Revolutionary War) but this fact did "not absolve them of the duty of mutual assistance that

nature imposes on individuals."[46] Therefore, natural law in the international arena must rightly

be consented to by all civilized nations if all were to prosper. This sentiment struck a chord

with Americas' founding fathers, who wanted to see their nation quickly rise to world

prominence, bud did not want to rely on the European traditions of using armed aggression

and the establishments of strong military alliances in order to ensure the country's ability to

enforce its claims to natural law. From that point forward, America was committed to

attempting to achieve a balance of power based on diplomacy, treaties, and an adherence to

natural law as part of a mutually agreed international standard.

In order to achieve a balance of power through observance of natural law, the United

States stressed "that the real interests of nations were harmonious,"[47] rather than aggressive.

Although war was permissible under Vattel's interpretation of natural law (indeed, under all

interpretations), his view provided for war only if a nation were to become belligerent or fell

under the control of a hegemonic ruler who could threaten the balance of power provided by

natural law. In order to achieve harmony, however, the United States set out to secure treaties instead of relying on alliances and monarchical assumptions. By doing so, "optimistic Revolutionaries therefore expected treaties they negotiated to play a crucial role in launching a 'new chapter in the laws of nations.'" Americans hoped that "by accepting" the terms and limitations set forth by its model treaties, they would "simultaneously endorse universally applicable" principles of natural law.[48] It was hoped, too, that these treaties, based on "friendship" and "free communication," would allow nations to "gradually attain a higher level of civility and morality in their relations."[49]

Immediately after the Revolution, the United States began to propagate treaties that sought to balance legal principle with maritime interests. Since it was thought that the ocean was a shared resource provided by divine providence, many of the first treaties sought by the United States with foreign nations were designed to secure navigation rights, through "stock" clauses, which stipulated navigations rights in international waters in an effort to ensure that these clauses would act as a "substitute for norms of universal international law."[50] Other "stock" clauses that were almost immediately utilized in American treaties were designed to secure friendship between the treaty nations, "most favored nation" status, protection of vessels from illegal search and seizure, and the protection of "admitted aliens and their property in the admitting state's territory."[51] In other words, early American treaties, which helped define the international standard for treaties, echoed the sentiment of the Rules of Oleron, propagated over seven hundred years in the past.

Standard Clauses in American Treaties

Many examples of "stock" clauses appear over and over again in American diplomatic history. Between nations of "civilized" standing, these provisions were fundamental acknowledgements of each nation's right to pursue commercial and diplomatic relationships on equal terms with one another. These nations' "civilized" status allowed for each to have equal treaty stipulations, because each signatory was demonstrating that they respected the other nation's standing as an influential mercantile nation with capable merchant fleets, powerful armies, and the political acumen necessary to negotiate effective treaties and to ensure that those treaty stipulations could be enforced. In essence, equal treaty stipulations confirmed that each nation viewed the other as "civilized." For example, the Treaty of Amity and Commerce Between the United States and France, signed on 6 February 1778 contained these articles:

> **Article I:** There shall be a firm, inviolable and universal Peace, and a true and sincere Friendship between the most Christian King, his Heirs and Successors, and the United States of America; and the Subjects of the most Christian King and of the said States; and between the Countries, Islands, Cities, and Towns, situate under the Jurisdiction of the most Christian King, and of the said United States, and the people and Inhabitants of every Degree, without exception of Persons or Places; & the Terms herein after mentioned shall be perpetual between the most Christian King his Heirs and Successors and the said United States.

> **Article II:** The most Christian King, and the United States engage mutually not to grant any particular Favor to other Nations in respect of Commerce and Navigation, which shall not immediately become common to the other Party, who shall enjoy the same Favor freely, if the Concession was freer made, or on allowing the same Compensation, if the Concession was Conditional.

> **Article VI:** The most Christian King shall endeavour by all the means in his Power to protect and defend all Vessels and the Effects belonging to the Subjects, People or Inhabitants of the said United States, or any of them, being in his Ports Havens or Roads or on the Sea near to his Countries, Islands Cities or Towns and to recover and restore to the right owners, their agents or Attornies all such Vessel & Effects, which shall be taken within his Jurisdiction; and the Ships of War of his most Christian Majesty or any Convoys sailing under his authority shall upon all Occasions take under their Protection all Vessels belonging to the Subjects, People or Inhabitants of the said United States, or any of them & holding the same Course or going the same Way, and

shall defend such Vessels, as long as they hold the same Course or go the same way, against all Attacks, Force and Violence in the same manner, as they ought to protect and defend the Vessels belonging to the Subjects of the most Christian King.

Article VII: In like manner the said United States and their Ships of War sailing under their Authority shall protect and defend, conformable to the Tenor of the preceding Article, all the Vessels and Effect belonging to the Subjects of the most Christian King; and use al their Endeavours to recover cause to be restored the said Vessels and Effects, that shall have been taken within the Jurisdiction of the said United State or any of them.

Article XVIII: All Ships and Merchandizes of what Nature soever which shall be rescued out of the hands of any Pirates or Robbers on the high Seas, shall be brought into some Port of either State and shall be delivered to the Custody of the Officers of that Port, in order to be restored entire to the true Proprietor, as soon as due and sufficient Proof shall be made concerning the Property thereof.

These "stock" treaty stipulations also appeared in treaties created with non-Western and non-Christian nations that were not part of the "civilized" group, because according to universal law theory, they applied to all humanity, however, such treaties, like the two secured with Japan by Matthew C. Perry and Townsend Harris, also included "unequal" clauses, which were meant to afford the "civilized" partner nation the treaty terms and stipulations it was accustomed to, while holding the "uncivilized" nation to more of a junior partner status. In essence, the "civilized" nation was asserting that the "uncivilized" partner nation had the rights to universally standardized trading arrangements, but that the "civilized" signatory did not yet trust that the "uncivilized" nation to have the power, experience, governmental authority, judicial system, or religious and social values necessary to ensure that the enforcement of all universal laws could be accomplished. Thus, clauses were added to give American citizens protection from "uncivilized" or "un-universal" native laws and judicial proceedings and provided compensation for damaged property.

The Treaty of Amity and Commerce Between Siam and the United States, signed on 20 March 1833, is an example of an unequal treaty designed to protect American interests:

"Equal" clauses included:

> **Article I:** There shall be a perpetual Peace between the Maginificent King of Siam and the United States of America

> **Article II:** The Citizens of the United States shall have free liberty to enter all the Ports of the Kingdom of Siam, with their cargoes, of whatever kind the said cargoes may consist; and they shall have liberty to sell the same to any of the subjects of the King, or others who may wish to purchase the same, or to barter the same for any produce or manufacture of the Kingdom, or other articles that may be found there.

> **Article V:** If any vessel of the United States shall suffer shipwreck on any part of the Magnificent King's dominions, the persons escaping from the wreck shall be taken care of and hospitably entertained at the expense of the King, until they shall find an opportunity to be returned to their country; and the property saved from such wreck shall be carefully preserved and restored to its owners; and the United States will repay all expenses incurred by His Majesty on account of such wreck.

> **Article IV:** If hereafter the Duties payable by foreign vessels be diminished in favour of any other nation, the same diminution shall be made in favour of the vessels of the United States.

> **Article VII:** If any citizens of the United States, or their vessels, or other property, shall be taken by pirates and brought within the dominions of the Magnificent King, the persons shall be set at liberty, and the property restored to its owners.

As United States could not yet trust that Siam's sovereign would be able to guarantee protection for American citizens or hassle-free trade, "unequal" articles designed to protect American interests were included, as well:

> **Article III ("fixed tariff" clause):** Vessels from the United States entering any Port within His Majesty's dominions, and selling or purchasing cargoes of merchandise, shall pay in lieu of import and export duties, tonnage, license to trade, or any other charge whatever, a measurement duty only, as follows: (measurement specifications follow)

Article IV ("most favored nation" clause): If hereafter the Duties payable by foreign vessels by diminished in favour of any other nation, the same diminution shall be made in favour of the vessels of the United States.

Article VIII (provided protection from pirates technically under the dominion of Siam's sovereign—a loose "indemnity" clause): If any citizens of the United States, or their vessels, or other property, shall be taken by pirates and brought within the dominions of the Magnificent King, the persons shall be set at liberty, and the property restored to its owners.

And, once again, the United States secured similar rights with China after the signing

of the Treaty of Wangxia, on 3 July 1844:

Article I: There shall be a perfect, permanent, universal peace, and a sincere and cordial amity, between the United States of American on the one part, and the Ta Tsing Empire on the other part, and between their people respectively, without exception of persons or places.

Article II (unequal): Citizens of the United States resorting to China for the purposes of commerce will pay the duties of import and export prescribed in the Tariff, which is fixed by and made a part of this Treaty. They shall, in no case, be subject to other higher duties than are or shall be required of the people of any other nature whatever.

Article V: At each of the [commerce ports], citizens of the United States lawfully engaged in commerce, shall be permitted to import from their own or any other ports into China, and sell there, and purchase therein, and export to their own or any other ports, all manner of merchandize, of which the importation or exportation is not prohibited by this Treaty…

Article XXI (unequal): Subjects of China who may be guilty of any criminal act towards citizens of the United States, shall be arrested and punished by the Chinese authorities according to the laws of China: and citizens of the United States, who may commit any crime in China, shall be subject to be tried and punished only by the Consul, or other public functionary of the United States, thereto authorized according to the laws of the United States.

Article XXVII: If any vessel of the United States shall be wrecked or stranded on the coast of China, and be subjected to plunder or other damage, the proper officers of government on received information of the fact, will immediately adopt measure for their relief and security; and the persons on board shall received friendly treatment, and be enabled at once to repair to the most convenient of the free ports, and shall enjoy all facilities for obtaining supplies of provisions and water. And if a vessel shall be forced in whatever way to take refuge in any port other than one of the free ports, then in like manner, the persons on board shall receive friendly treatment, and the means of safety and security.

Article XXVIII: Citizens of the United States, their vessels and property, shall not be subject to any embargo; nor shall they be seized or forcibly be detained for any pretense of the public service; but they shall be suffered to prosecute their commerce in a quiet, and without molestation or embarrassment.

Unequal treaties were acceptable under the tenets of natural law. In his seminal work on the matter, *The Law of Nations* (1758), Emmerich de Vattel specifically addressed the matter of unequal treaties in the twelfth chapter of his second book, "Of Treaties of Alliance, and Other Public Treaties." Specifically, section 175, entitled "Unequal Treaties and Unequal Alliances," Vattel notes that tradition afforded "great potentates...a superiority of honors and respect" from a "weak state."[52] He explained that "a great monarch" would often offer the weaker state "advantageous conditions" such as "gratuitous succors," "assistance of all his forces," or "assistance gratis," and in return, expected "respect from his ally" and was allowed to claim "a superiority of dignity." In other words, there is an implicit bond between the stronger and weaker state. The stronger state agrees to allow the weaker state access to its resources, especially its market and goods (and possibly its military), while the weaker state respects the stronger state for allowing it into a partnership. In the context of treaties of amity and commerce, the weaker state respects the stronger state's overall military, economic, and cultural position, and its ability to afford a larger measure of these to the weaker state than the weaker state could provide to the stronger.

Stronger nations, such as the United States, who felt compelled, "by necessity," to intervene in a weaker or belligerent country's affairs through a demonstration of military force or excessive political pressure, were allowed to impose "burdensome… oppressive or disagreeable conditions." Treaty stipulations such as "most favored nation" clauses, extraterritoriality, and fixed tariffs were a direct outgrowth of this ideal. Vattel acknowledged that these types of treaties demeaned the weaker state and forced it acknowledge "[its] own inferiority," while, "at the same time…exalts…[the] more powerful ally." Section 181 argues that unequal treaties are "consistent with justice" to "render [an aggressor] incapable of easily injuring" another nation. Vattel argued, in section 177, that these types of unequal treaties were to be avoided, and only used if "such measures" were "necessary for the preservation" of either the weaker or stronger nation. Vattel also argued in section 180 that unequal treaties were valid under natural law, because the "care of [a nation's] own safety" were valid concerns.

Conclusion

The men who formulated Matthew Calbraith Perry's mission to Japan, then, were at a crossroads in American history. The businessmen, politicians, and naval officers who promoted the Perry mission were the children of three philosophical parents that influenced them greatly. The first parent that helped conceive the Perry mission was one anchored in the growing relevancy of mid-nineteenth century American forms of humanism, which believed in the power and sovereignty of the individual to become "moral and good" because it was in his or her nature to do so. This ideal rests on the foundation of the "unified theory of power," which assumed that God divinely-empowered individuals to hold within themselves the capacity for self-rule within their own household, but also the responsibility to empower the government and to change its laws, if necessary.

The second parent was the Americans' ability to connect commerce to their humanitarian ideals. No longer was an individual's economic success tied to feudal lords or merchants who controlled commercial interests; rather individuals, and more precisely men, had the ability to form commercial connections with whomever they pleased. These connections, if administered properly, would benefit both parties, and at the same time, would add to the humanitarian repertoire of all the actors involved. Commercial interactions also promoted the solidification of "polite" society, as individuals were compelled to adhere to behavioral standards that promoted honest, productive commerce, while, at the same time, discouraging selfish or harmful modes of conduct.

The third source of American ideals was the interpretation of natural law that helped spawn the American Revolution. Statements such as the 1774 Declaration of the first Continental Congress, which asserts that the "immutable laws of nature" give men and polities "certain rights," or the Declaration of Independence, which stated that people are vested with "the Laws of Nature," which were created by "Nature's God," demonstrate that, to the founding fathers, natural law was real, and tangible, and was given to mankind by divine rights.[53] Americans purposely attempted to forge a balance of power by replacing traditional military alliances and agreements between monarchs with a form of natural law that considered all nations both distinct entities, linked through divine providence that aggregated the material blessings and developments from all nations, civilized or not. This ideal was based on long-standing legal and maritime tradition and was spawned by the Greek notion of the city-state nearly two millennia prior to the founding of the United States.

NOTES FOR CHAPTER IV

1. Mary Beth Norton, *Founding Mothers and Father: Gendered Power and the Forming of American Society* (New York: A. A. Knopf, 1996), 8.

2. Ibid.

3. Ibid.

4. Noll, "Introduction," 3, 7.

5. Ibid., 12.

6. Ibid., 7.

7. Mark A. Noll, "Protestant Reasoning about Money and the Economy, 1790-1860: A Preliminary Probe," *God and Mammon: Protestants, Money, and the Market, 1790-1860,* ed. Mark A Noll (New York: Oxford University Press, 2002), 265.

8. Ibid.

9. Ibid.

10. Methodism in the North later veered toward formalism, however. See Noll, "Introduction," 12.

11. Noll, "Introduction," 12.

12. Daniel Walker Howe, "Charles Sellers, the Market Revolution, and the Shaping of Identity in Whig-Jacksonian America," *God and Mammon: Protestants, Money, and the Market, 1790-1860,* ed. Mark A Noll (New York: Oxford University Press, 2002), 56.

13. Louise Stephenson, *Scholarly Means to Evangelical Ends: The New Haven Scholars and the Transformation of Higher Learning in America, 1830-1890* (Baltimore: Johns Hopkins University Press, 1986), 5-6.

14. Howe, 63.

15. Ibid.

16. Ibid., 63-4.

17. Ibid., 65.

18. Ibid.

19. Anne C. Rose, *Voices of the Marketplace: American Thought and Culture, 1830-1860* (New York: Maxwell Macmillan International, 1995), xvi-xvii.

20. A useful discussion of politeness and Victorian American society can be found in Kasson, Rudeness & Civility.

21. Howe, 66.

22. Ibid.

23. John Daniel Wild, *Plato's Modern Enemies and the Theory of Natural Law* (Chicago: University of Chicago Press, 1953), 71.

24. Ibid., 64.

25. Ibid., 65.

26. Chris Brown, Terry Nardin, and Nicholas Rengger, eds., *International Relations in Political Thought: Texts From the Ancient Greeks to the First World War* (New York: Cambridge University Press, 2002), 1.

27. Ibid.

28. "Japan—the Expedition," *The American Whig Review, 508.*

29. Wild, 71.

30. James Brown Scott, *Law, the State, and the International Community: A Commentary on the Development of Legal, Political, and International Ideals,* vol. 1 (New York: Columbia University Press, 1939), 54. Other relevant works on the development of law: Fred Miller Jr., *Nature, Justice, and Right in Aristotle's Politics* (Oxford: Clarendon Press, 1995) and Geoffrey Butler and Simon Maccoby, *The Development of International Law* (London: Longmans Green and Co. LTD., 1928).

31. Ibid.

32. Ibid., 93. Other works concerning Stoic ideals applied to natural law is Malcolm Schofield, *The Stoic Idea of the City* (New York: Cambridge University Press, 1991);.

33. Ibid., 94.

34. Ibid., 95.

35. Ibid., 97.

36. Ibid., 98.

37. Ibid.

38. Ibid.

39. See R. F. Wright, *Medieval Internationalism: The Contributions of the Medieval Church to International Law and Peace* (London: Williams & Norgate, LTD., 1930), 183-210.

40. This translation is at: "Admiralty and Maritime Law Guide – Rules of Oleron," n.d., <http://www.admiraltylawguide.com/documents/oleron.html> (12 March 2005).

41. Wright, 208.

42. Onuf and Onuf, Federal Union, Modern World, 4-5. Another treatment of the development of American thought in regards to natural law is Francis Stephen Ruddy, *International Law in the Enlightenment: The Background of Emmerich de Vattel's Le Droit Des Gens* (Dobbs Ferry, New York: Oceana Publications, Inc., 1975).

43. Peter S. Onuf and Nicholas Greenwood Onuf, *Federal Union, Modern World: The Law of Nations in an Age of Revolutions, 1776-1814* (Madison: Madison House, 1993), 11.

44. Scott, 267.

45. Brown, Nardin, et. al., 322.

46. Onuf and Onuf, 16.

47. Ibid., 111.

48. Ibid.

49. Ibid., 112-13.

50. Arthur Nussbaum, *A Concise history of the Law of Nations* (New York: Macmillan Co., 1947), 201.

51. Robert Renbert Wilson, *The International Law Standard in Treaties of the United States* (Cambridge: Harvard University Press), 88.

52. A copy of this section can be found at Emmerich de Vattel, "de Vattel: Of Treaties of Alliance, and Other Public Treaties" in *The Laws of Nature and Nature's God,* n.d. <http://www.lonang.com/exlibris/vattel/vatt-212.htm> (2 April 2005).

53. See Scott, 266.

CONCLUSION

This study has attempted to lay the groundwork for a re-interpretation of the political, social, economic, religious, and cultural attitudes that helped shape United States policy toward Japan in the mid-nineteenth century. Although economic considerations for the mission were decidedly present, there has been a general failure to recognize that the nineteenth century Western worldview centered on morals, ethics, and standards of propriety that are just as foreign to many contemporary Westerners as Japan was to men like Perry, Glynn, and Fillmore. However, since the bulk of the research into the Perry mission was completed, historians have been continually working to better understand the antebellum worldview. Thus, research into the Perry mission to become stagnant and has fallen behind more recent studies of the greater social, cultural, political, legal, and economic ideologies of influential individuals who proposed, lobbied for, and authorized the mission to Japan.

In order for this reinterpretation to lay the proper groundwork for future studies, it is important to determine how to reintegrate commercial considerations into the larger whole. Historian David F. Long provides such a foundation for the role of commerce and commercial considerations as they relate to overseas concerns. In his 1988 study of American naval officers' duties as both military commanders and regional *charges d'affairs,* Long pointed out that naval officers had flexible job descriptions granted to them by their governments in order to effectively carry out diplomacy and to protect national interests far from their home waters, with no means to quickly dispatch messages and wait for orders on how to proceed. In essence, naval officers were charged with an enormous burden that mirrored the best and the worst of

their nation's foreign policy and the men charged to enact it.

> [A naval officer] had many duties to perform beyond his obvious one of keeping his ship and people in fighting trim. In wartime he battled against Frenchmen, north Africans, Britons, Mexican, and his fellow-American Confederates. Sometimes he was assigned the leadership of exploration expeditions in which he had to pay careful attention to marine soundings and coastal surveys…The officer occasionally acted as a humanitarian, rescuing castaways of all nationalities and landing at ports to quell fires. Sometimes he had to behave as a policeman, protecting sea lands from pirate and going ashore to restore order during foreign insurrections or outbreaks of mob violence; now and then he brought refugees on board for transportation to safety. He was known to save missionaries from outraged natives, particularly in the Middle and Far East. While commanding a squadron he continually circulated form port to port throughout his jurisdiction, "showing the flag" to assure Americans living abroad that their country was concerned about their personas and property, in addition to remind foreigners of U.S. power. In all of these occupations, however, officers followed a single lodestar: the protection and enhancement of the nation's commerce. [1]

The term loadstar is apropos, as economic concerns acted as a guide for naval activities, but it

was not the sole concern. Ships and the men that plied their trades onboard provided a service

to a nation that could be measured in tangible ways. Thus, a merchant marine fleet was

directly linked to commerce, for without the latter, the former would only exist for the sake of

scientific inquiry or possibly to transport individuals who did not have the means cross an

ocean's great expanses. Without economic interest, there would hardly be need for great fleets

such as the one that hunted whales off the coast of Hokkaido. With this in mind, future

inquiry into the origins of the Perry mission must seek to view the events surrounding the

men of the *Lawrence* and *Lagoda* as a part of a larger whole that takes into account the prevailing

worldviews of the participants involved in the decision making process. Commerce drove

decision makers, but opening Japan's markets to American commerce was only one of the factors in the eventual play between Perry and the Japanese officials near the shores of Kanagawa.

In addition to social, political, legal, and religious factors, one of the primary forces dictating the reaction of the U.S. government to Japan was the continuation of a standing practice for nations to protect its citizens to the best of its ability, whether that ability be in the realm of politics, the military, or both. The reactions, however carried forth, were the product of laws and accepted rules of conduct developed over hundreds, if not thousands. of years and their study spans a multitude of historical disciplines ranging from legal to religious, and cultural to philosophical. By seeing the Perry mission as a portion of a larger whole, the event appears not to be the product of an incremental and ad-hoc design by American business concerns working in relative seclusion, but as an evolutionary step in the United States' continuing efforts to ensure that its citizens, whether engaged in commerce, trade, religious missions, or traveling for the mere sake of pleasure, were safe and afforded the confidence that their government, with all its military and diplomatic power, had not abandoned them. If viewed in this manner, Perry's mission to Japan was not out of the ordinary, though it may been more dramatic and less violent than similar missions that came decades, and even centuries before it. Indeed, Perry's mission brought to Japan more gratuitous displays of Western, and particularly, American, culture and technology than was originally planned by the mission's original commander, John H. Aulick, who did not bring with him a steam engine and passenger cars, a telegraph, minstrel bands, or chefs of the highest caliber; all he took with him was President Fillmore's letter, castaways to return to Japan, and the diplomatic power he had been assigned to use.

However, for a great many historians, especially Japanists and Asianists, imagining Perry's mission to Japan as a mere continuation of standard diplomatic procedure is quite difficult, for soon after Perry's departure, Japan's future was dramatically and irrevocably changed by the upheavals within Japanese society that led to rioting, civil war, and an eventual overthrow of a government that had been in place for nearly 250 years. Thus, there is no doubt that in the context of U.S.-Japan relations and Japanese history, the event is momentous, but in the context of U.S. history, up until that time, the Perry mission to Japan and the subsequent treaties that followed were, more or less, standard applications of commonly applied maritime laws and treaty goals, and possibly somewhat uninteresting or pedestrian when viewed as a mere piece of maritime history.

But, in the end, history, and this study, is left with whalers from the ships *Lawrence* and *Lagoda*, who have found themselves continually at the center of a historical debate that has not entirely determined what to credit them with. Were they merely pawns in the game of chess played by politicians, businessmen, and naval officers, or were the legitimate victims of an isolated government filled with suspicion and frightened of the prospect of an invasion by a Western power? Were they uncultured and uncivilized ruffians who had little regard for their captors' instructions, or were they frightened victims of circumstance who resorted to drastic measures because they felt that their future was so uncertain that they had no other choice?

The sailors were the focal point of those who, at the time and on both sides of the ocean, tried their best to protect their traditions, social mores, commercial interests, and people. Men such as Perry and Fillmore were concerned with upholding their duties to their citizens as required by popular consent and set forth previously in legal and maritime traditions commonly interpreted through the lens of *natural law*. Influencing their decisions was a new wave of humanitarian concern, Victorian ideals, and ambient, but pervasive, religious influences that worked continually to alter the hearts and minds of those creating and implementing foreign policies.

NOTES FOR CONCLUSION

1. David F. Long, *Gold Braid and Foreign Relations: Diplomatic Activities of U.S. Naval Officers, 1798-1883* (Annapolis: Naval Institute Press, 1988), 8-9.

BIBLIOGRAPHY

Government Documents

Correspondence Relative to the Naval Expedition to Japan. United States Senate, 33rd Congress, 2nd Session, Senate Executive Document 34.

Imprisoned American Seamen. United States House of Representatives, 31st Congress, 1st Session, Executive Document 84.

Official Documents Relative to the Naval Expedition to Japan. United States Senate, 32nd Congress, 1st Session, Executive Document 59.

Unpublished Manuscripts, Theses, and Dissertations

Borst, William Adam. "The American Merchant and the Genesis of Japanese-American Commercial Relations, 1790-1858." Ph.D. diss., Saint Louis University, 1972.

Hamlin, F. H. 1907. A forgotten naval expedition and something of its commander, James Glynn. Paper read before the Canandaigua Scientific Association (Canandaigua, New York), 8 October.

Honeycutt, William C. "The Early Political Career of Charles Magill Conrad." M.A. thesis, The Louisiana State University and A&M College, 1939.

Humeston, Helen. "Origins of America's Japan Policy, 1790-1854." Ph.D. diss., University of Minnesota, 1981.

Newspapers and Miscellaneous Documents

"Admiralty and Maritime Law Guide – Rules of Oleron." n.d., <http://www.admiraltylawguide.com/documents/oleron.html> (12 March 2005).

Seaman's Friend of Honolulu, 1 December 1848

Books and Articles

Barre, W. L. *The Life and Public Services of Millard Fillmore.* Buffalo: Wanzer, McKim, and Co., 1856.

Brown, Chris, Terry Nardin, and Nicholas Rengger, eds. *International Relations in Political Thought: Texts From the Ancient Greeks to the First World War.* New York: Cambridge University Press, 2002.

Butler, Geoffrey and Simon Maccoby. *The Development of International Law.* London: Longmans Green and Co. LTD., 1928.

Dennett, Tyler. *Americans in East Asia: A Critical Study of the Policy of the United States with Reference to China, Japan, and Korea in the 19th Century.* New York: Macmillan Co., 1922.

Duus, Peter. The Japanese Discovery of America: A Brief History with Documents. Boston: Bedford Books, 1997.

Grayson, Benson Lee. *The Unknown President: The Administration of President Millard Fillmore* Washington: University Press of American, 1981.

Howe, Daniel Walker. "Charles Sellers, the Market Revolution, and the Shaping of Identity in Whig-Jacksonian America." In *God and Mammon: Protestants, Money, and the Market, 1790-1860,* 54-73. Edited by Mark A. Noll. New York: Oxford University Press, 2002.

"The Japan Expedition and its Results." *The United States Democratic Review* 32, no 1 (1853): 64-80.

"Japan—the Expedition." *The American Whig Review* 15, no. 90 (1852): 507-16.

Johnson, Robert Erwin. *Far China Station: The U.S. Navy in Asian Waters, 1800-1898.* Annapolis: Naval Institute Press, 1979.

Lewis, William S. and Naojiro Murakami. *Ranald MacDonald: The Narrative of His Early Life on the Columbia Under the Hudson's Bay Company's Regime; of His Experiences in the Pacific Whale Fishery; and of His Great Adventure to Japan'; With a Sketch of His Later Life on the Western Frontier, 1824-1894.* Portland: Oregon Historical Society Press, 1990.

Long, David F. *Gold Braid and Foreign Relations: Diplomatic Activities of U.S. Naval Officers, 1798-1883.* Annapolis: Naval Institute Press, 1988.

Miller, Fred, Jr. *Nature, Justice, and Right in Aristotle's Politics.* Oxford: Clarendon Press, 1995.

Morison, Samuel Elliot. *"Old Bruin": The Life of Commodore Matthew C. Perry, 1794-1858.* Boston: Little, Brown and Company, 1967.

Neumann, William L. "Religion, Morality, and Freedom: The Ideological Background of the Perry Expedition." *Pacific Historical Review* 28, no. 3 (1954): 247-57.

Noll, Mark A. "Introduction." In *God and Mammon: Protestants, Money, and the Market, 1790-1860,* 3-29. Edited by Mark A. Noll. New York: Oxford University Press, 2002.

——————. "Protestant Reasoning about Money and the Economy, 1790-1860: A Preliminary Probe." In *God and Mammon: Protestants, Money, and the Market, 1790-1860,* 265-294. Edited by Mark A. Noll. New York: Oxford University Press, 2002.

Norton, Mary Beth. *Founding Mothers and Father: Gendered Power and the Forming of American Society.* New York: A. A. Knopf, 1996.

Nussbaum, Arthur. *A Concise history of the Law of Nations.* New York: Macmillan Co., 1947.

Offutt, Milton. *The Protection of Citizens Abroad by the Armed Forces of the United States.* Baltimore: Johns Hopkins University Press, 1928.

Onuf, Peter S. and Nicholas Greenwood Onuf. *Federal Union, Modern World: The Law of Nations in an Age of Revolutions, 1776-1814.* Madison: Madison House, 1993.

Palmer, Aaron Haight. *Documents and Facts Illustrating the Origin of the Mission to Japan.* Washington: Henry Polkhorn, 1857.

Perry, John Curtis. *Facing West: Americans and the Opening of the Pacific.* Westport, Conn.: Praeger, 1994.

Plummer, Katherine. *The Shogun's Reluctant Ambassadors: Japanese Sea Drifters in the North Pacific.* Portland: Oregon Historical Society Press, 1991.

Rayback, Robert J. *Millard Fillmore: Biography of a President.* Buffalo: Buffalo Historical Society, 1959.

Roe, Jo Ann. *Ranald MacDonald: Pacific Rim Adventurer.* Pullman: Washington State University Press, 1997.

Rose, Anne C. *Voices of the Marketplace: American Thought and Culture, 1830-1860.* New York: Maxwell Macmillan International, 1995.

Ruddy, Francis Stephen. *International Law in the Enlightenment: The Background of Emmerich de Vattel's Le Droit Des Gens.* Dobbs Ferry, New York: Oceana Publications, Inc., 1975.

Sakamaki, Shunzo. *Japan and the United States: A Study of Japanese Contacts with and Conceptions of the United States and Its People Prior to the American Expedition of 1853-4.* Tokyo: Asiatic Society of Japan, 1939.

Scarry, Robert J. *Millard Fillmore.* Jefferson, N.C.: McFarland, 2001.

Schofield, Malcolm. *The Stoic Idea of the City.* New York: Cambridge University Press, 1991.

Schroeder, John H. *Matthew Calbraith Perry: Antebellum Sailor and Diplomat.* Annapolis: Naval Institute Press, 2001.

—————————. *Shaping a Maritime Empire: The Commercial and Diplomatic Role of the American Navy, 1829-1861.* Westport, Conn.: Greenwood Press, 1985.

Scott, James Brown. *Law, the State, and the International Community: A Commentary on the Development of Legal, Political, and International Ideals,* vol. 1. New York: Columbia University Press, 1939.

Stephenson, Louise. *Scholarly Means to Evangelical Ends: The New Haven Scholars and the Transformation of Higher Learning in America, 1830-1890.* Baltimore: Johns Hopkins University Press, 1986.

Tower, Walter Sheldon. *A History of the American Whale Fishery.* Philadelphia: The University of Pennsylvania Press, 1907.

De Vattel, Emmerich. "de Vattel: Of Treaties of Alliance, and Other Public Treaties." *The Laws of Nature and Nature's God.* n.d. <http://www.lonang.com/exlibris/vattel/vatt-212.htm> (2 April 2005).

Wakabayashi, Bob Tadashi. *Anti-foreignism and Western Learning in Early-modern Japan: The New Thesis of 1825.* Cambridge, Mass.: Council on East Asian Studies, Harvard University, 1986.

—————————————. "Opium, Expulsion, Sovereignty, China's Lessons for Bakumatsu Japan." *Monumenta Nipponica* 47, no. 1 (1992): 1-25.

Wild, John Daniel. *Plato's Modern Enemies and the Theory of Natural Law.* Chicago: University of Chicago Press, 1953.

Wildes, Harry Emerson. *Aliens in the East: A New History of Japan's Foreign Intercourse.* Philadelphia: University of Pennsylvania Press, 1937.

Wiley, Peter Booth and Korogi Ichiro. *Yankees in the Land of the Gods: Commodore Petty and the Opening of Japan.* New York: Viking, 1990.

Wilson, Robert Renbert. *The International Law Standard in Treaties of the United States.* Cambridge: Harvard University Press.

Wright, R. F. *Medieval Internationalism: The Contributions of the Medieval Church to International Law and Peace.* London: Williams & Norgate, LTD., 1930.

www.ingramcontent.com/pod-product-compliance
Lightning Source LLC
Chambersburg PA
CBHW080420290526
45791CB00008BA/2358